In the Driving Seat of Customer Experience

In the Driving Seat of Customer Experience

with Customer Signals Management

Zanna van der Aa

Warden Press

© 2020 Zanna van der Aa

ISBN: 978-94-92004-91-8

Original title: *Klantsignaalmanagement. Stap voor stap naar een meetbare klantbeleving* (Culemborg: Van Duuren Management, 2016). Translated from the Dutch by Debbie Baker. Previously published as *Customer Signals Management. In the Driving Seat of Customer Experience* (Amsterdam: Warden Press, 2017).

Cover design: Roquefort Ontwerpers, Utrecht
Photo author: Tatiana Leijn, Arnhem
Interior design and layout: Holland Graphics, Amsterdam

This edition published by Warden Press, Amsterdam

TABLE OF CONTENTS

FOREWORD BY THE AUTHOR

Towards the end of 2004, it suddenly occurred to me: "Wouldn't it be great if organizations could be convinced that treating people in the right way (in this case customers and employees) was profitable? Hmm, but who's going to listen to Zanna from Arnhem? Board members are unlikely to be convinced without some degree of research to prove it... Hmm... a doctorate...? Yeuch, a doctorate..." This reaction stemmed from my conviction that there is a yawning gap between science and day-to-day practice. And my aim was precisely to reach the latter. One thing I knew for certain was that I was unwilling to conduct research within the university system, and instead – if at all – it would need to be done parallel to my work as an organizational advisor. Off I headed with my comprehensive yet insistent list of requirements, to confer with Professor Dr. José Bloemer of Radboud University in Nijmegen. She had mentored me during graduation, in (customer) complaints management. After meeting three times, she was convinced of the scientific merit and I was convinced that this potential ordeal (yes, I knew that beforehand) was indeed the route required in order to achieve my practical target. My then manager at CapGemini, Maarten Veldhuizen, subsequently saw fit to grant me one day in the week for my research (for which I'm eternally grateful), and I officially became an 'external doctorate candidate'.

My aim was to prove that three mutually reinforcing spearheads are vital for successful organizations: committed customers, committed employees and continuous improvement. The context within which I was able to prove this, was that of the customer contact environment: the contact center. At that time, such centers were a source of great customer dissatisfaction, and turnover of employees was a major issue. As a department however, the contact center sits on a veritable crock of gold in terms of data deployable for continuous improvement of the organization from the customer's perspective. My chosen scope of branches were those which affected me as a consumer or citizen in the case of their failure: healthcare insurers, banks, government institutions and telecom.

For me, the most enjoyable part of the process was the practical research, looking behind the scenes at many organizations. And although my motivation was already 100 percent, it was boosted to 300 percent following the initial sessions with customers and employees. While there were many reasons for this, with hindsight there were two leitmotifs which struck me in particular. The first was the signals gained from these sessions, that customers felt themselves to be ignored by organizations. There was a sense of powerlessness when faced with a large organization. Employees also regularly indicated that they received no further reaction to their feedback regarding the need for improvement. The second leitmotif which energized me tremendously, was the commitment by everyone involved to proactively assist in the improvement process. Although both parties certainly also vented their frustration, a U-turn was made within the same session, to thinking along and making useful suggestions for the organization. I became aware of the potential of connecting the three parties – customer, employer and organization – which is still my motivation for getting up each morning.

When referring to meaning, which is one of the most important elements for employee satisfaction, one aspect will always be meaningful for me: the constant search for connection between customers, employees and the organization. Throw in the complex puzzle (read: amazing challenge) of achieving this in practice while continually developing the method to include new insight, and you have found my incentive to embrace customer signals management. The creativity to re-examine what is effective in this specific context for this specific problem, day in day out. The need for continuous self-examination in order to fulfil the advisory role as genuinely as possible. The sensitivity not to judge people but rather to truly comprehend where they stand and to discover how they can be mobilized. The creation of pragmatism and simplicity from the customer's perspective, to generate the energy required to work together. And the last but possibly not least explanation for the success of initiatives in the field of customer signals management: establishment of a connection by coupling customer experience to the language of the organization, to render the customer experience steerable via customer satisfaction and cost efficiency. Instead of mere intentions, this therefore results in action being undertaken, with measurable results.

After a number of years working as an organizational advisor, I had the wonderful opportunity to prove all this in practice as a program manager at the Delta Lloyd insurance company from 2012 to 2015. The crux of the evidence I was hoping to provide was that costs can be dramatically cut by improving services from the customer's perspective – creating a win-win situation by raising customer satisfaction and lowering costs. By constantly examining and improving services from the customer's perspective, contact moments were reduced by more than 20 percent while simultaneously improving customer satisfaction. It was a fantastic, complex puzzle which we successfully solved as a team. A concerted effort, as there is no single egg of Columbus, it is Marketing which tempts customers online, Online which improves and innovates its services using tools such as a virtual assistant, Finance which changes its method of calculation, the Back Office which clarifies texts in communication, et cetera. All this was based on customer signals as the starting point, giving us valuable information on where improvements were required.

I still look back on that period with great affection and pleasure, having learned many valuable lessons about what works in practice, and what not. At the end of 2015, I translated a decade's worth of such lessons into this book. I hope you will enjoy putting the theory into practice just as much as I do, to take us another step towards greater customer centricity.

Zanna van der Aa
Huissen, July 2016

P.S. For anyone interested in the PhD ordeal cliffhanger... 6.5 years later, my brainchild was born: I received my title on 8 February 2012. Top of my list of compliments on that day came from Professor Dr. Hein van Duivenboden*, with whom I worked with great pleasure at CapGemini and had therefore requested that he become a member of the panel of expert examiners: "Never before have I encountered anyone whose thesis is as practically relevant as yours." The final year of my doctoral research was indeed an ordeal: processing all the results into scientifically justified articles, which I knew would never be read by anyone in the practical situation. However, I would do it all again, when considering the effect, in practice, of all my blogs, lectures and continuing interpretation of directly applicable concepts for organizations. I am also certain that it would never have come to fruition without the occasional loving and absolutely essential kick in my pants by husband Willem.

---

*   Sadly, Hein passed away much too young, from ALS, on 8 December 2014.

FOREWORD BY PROFESSOR DR. JOSÉ M.M. BLOEMER

Improve your organization's customer centricity with this unique, practically-oriented book on customer signals management.

We are all aware of the necessity of customer centricity. After all, there are plenty of examples of organizations all around us which fail to meet customers' expectations to one degree or another. All these missed opportunities offer an organization room for continuous improvement.

It will be clear that many of them struggle to find an approach to such an essential improvement. Where to begin and how to ensure you achieve results which customers will actually notice?

There are many books which can help you increase your organization's customer centricity. However, this book translates the daily customer experiences, employee services and their mutual involvement in the organization, into an approach for essential improvement. *Customer Signals Management* takes you by the hand, helping you to actually make your organization more customer centric and to avoid unnecessary customer contact. Improving customer centricity by means of reduced customer contact. At first glance, that sounds somewhat paradoxical. You may well be thinking: "Surely I need more customer contact in order to improve customer centricity? I can only satisfy customers by investing more time, effort and attention." However, most customers do not expect you to spend a great deal of time and attention on them. They are simply looking for efficient and especially effective assistance. And so reduced customer contact not only reduces costs accordingly, but also – more importantly – increases customer satisfaction and loyalty.

First and foremost, Zanna van der Aa is inspired and fueled by day-to-day practice. Her many years of successful practical experience enable her to very clearly describe what is required in order to enhance the customer experience of your organization.

As Zanna's professor and promoter, I know at first hand how motivated she is. While wishing to be inspired by science, her end goal is always to translate that science into good common sense (as she herself calls it). She is a woman on a mission, with the conviction to head straight for her target. I hope the advice, tips and tools she shares with you in this book will also serve as a source of inspiration for you. There is no standard solution after all. You have work to do. I have no doubt that you will do so successfully, thanks to this book.

Professor Dr. José M.M. Bloemer
Maastricht, 15 August 2016

INTRODUCTION

Choose a job you love, and you will never have to work a day in your life.
— CONFUCIUS

More and more organizations can be heard to despair: "We've looked into all kinds of things in recent years, and we also register the details of our customer contacts. We have a 'to do' list of improvements. Yet we're not making progress. So what are the smartest improvements we can make, with a measurable effect on our customers' experience? How can I show that customer experience can earn the organization money? And how do I get my entire organization to think and work from the customer's perspective?" Does this sound familiar? These are the key issues for customer signals management: an approach which renders customer experience steerable in terms of both customer satisfaction and cost efficiency.

Customer experience is trending!

Customer experience, customer engagement, customer centricity… All new terms which basically refer to the same problem: how can I gear the organization optimally to my customers' needs? The past 15 years have seen an encouraging change of tack. Back in the day, you needed to convince everyone of the fact that loyal customers earn a company money. By now, there is no end of proof that organizations which appreciate loyal customers and employees, outscore the competition who take them less seriously, on any number of financial attributes. There is therefore no longer any doubt about the importance of loyal customers and employees. The question has now shifted: "But how do I do it? How do I create such loyal customers? How do I create such loyal employees?" Customer experience is certainly here to stay at every organization in the next decade(s).

Yet it's tricky

The fact that there is attention for customer experience does not mean that organizations are automatically successful in improving it. Essentially, customer needs could not be simpler. We're all human, and it's hardly difficult to deduce how you yourself, your mother, your partner wants to be treated. Yet apparently it's not that easy. An organization is a complex entity of products, services, departments, processes, interests, et cetera, and all these aspects need to coalesce in order to improve customer experience. After all, a customer purchasing a new product deals with Online, with Customer Service, with Marketing, with the Back Office and with Finance. And somewhere in all these departments, there are employees writing copy for the website, answering the phone, devising a marketing campaign, writing the product manual, drawing up the invoice, and so on. Customer experience therefore affects the complete organization, which is what makes it such a fascinating and challenging puzzle.

Make it steerable

One of the most important principles lacking in many customer experience initiatives, is to speak the language of the organization: to render customer experience steerable. Most organizations know how to manage by numbers. If an organization is to become mobilized, it is essential to also create the right management information from the customer experience point of view. Customer signals management does so based on two mutually reinforcing perspectives:

1. Perspective number one is customer satisfaction. By designing customer satisfaction surveys according to the end-to-end customer journey (the steps taken by customers in passing through your organization) and the smart use of statistics, you can tell everyone exactly which knobs to turn. And therefore how you can best invest in improving customer satisfaction.
2. Perspective number two concerns avoidance of unnecessary customer contact. Avoiding such contact offers a win-win situation for customers and the organization alike. Customers don't want to call

you three times needlessly, and any contact avoided translates into direct cost savings for the organization.

By combining the two perspectives in customer signals management, you take the driving seat, steering and improving your organization's customer experience.

Clear focus in practice

Two interesting practical examples demonstrate how this management process works. A director of a social services department was convinced that submitting documentary proof when requesting supplementary benefit was a very tedious activity for customers. Initiatives had even been taken to adapt policy, to minimize the documents to be submitted. Upon designing a customer satisfaction survey regarding the application for supplementary benefit in terms of customer signals management, customers were asked how they valued this process and we were able to objectively measure the importance of this aspect. Not only was the impact shown to be low, in fact the required documents had no significant impact at all on satisfaction. Much more important was the letter giving the decision, and how quickly it was received.

In another organization, analysis of unnecessary customer contact not only cut this unnecessary customer contact by 25 percent (thus also substantially reducing costs), but at the same time boosted the customer satisfaction score from 7.4 to 7.9. By staying alert to missteps from the customer's perspective, you can discover a myriad of opportunities for improvement which positively and simultaneously influence both objectives.

Your personal adviser

After reading this book, you will be able to implement customer signals management in any organization. It has been designed as your personal adviser, taking you by the hand and showing you how to personally apply customer signals management successfully in organizations. After all, there is no standard method for each and every organization. You will need to deploy your own competences optimally in order to successfully apply customer signals management:

your creativity to get people on board this new initiative – and keep them there; your sensitivity to relate to all involved and to grasp what is going on; your self-reflection to remain conscious of your own role and where it is effective or not; your analytical capacity to apply the available data smartly for the right analyses; et cetera. All these factors play a role if you wish to mobilize the organization and truly improve customer services.

Reading Guide

The book has been compiled to follow the customer signals management approach: you start by determining the importance of customer experience for your organization (chapter 1) and by explaining the exact nature of customer signals management to those involved (chapter 2). All your subsequent actions are taken within the framework of the end-to-end customer journey (chapter 3). The framework helps you define the customer satisfaction knobs to be turned (chapter 4) and avoid unnecessary customer contact, resulting in cost reduction (chapter 5). On initiating customer signals management, you will soon discover many in-company myths and the fact that you require data to either rebut or confirm them from the customer perspective (chapter 6). Now that you have this insight, it can be put to work to improve services (chapter 7). At various points in the process, you will need to identify employee roles and how they can best be actively involved (chapter 8). And finally, you will read how to make a success of customer signals management (chapter 9) and the lessons learned in nearly ten years of applying this approach in practice (chapter 10). Make the most of it and add your own top lessons in the years to come!

1 THE RATIONALE OF CUSTOMER SIGNALS MANAGEMENT

Everything that irritates us about others, can lead us to an understanding of ourselves. — CARL GUSTAV JUNG

Customer signals management allows an organization's desire to become more customer centric, to be put into practice. More and more organizations have such a desire. Why is customer centricity gaining importance and what makes it so complex, for an organization, to achieve this?

1.1 Why is customer centricity an issue?

It is actually very strange that organizations struggle to gain insight into and relate to their customers' needs. It is the justification for their existence after all. This applies not only to commercial organizations, as the public sector equally runs the risk of losing tasks to other parties if they are not performed satisfactorily. So why is customer centricity an issue to start with?

Increasingly detached from customers
As soon as an organization employs more than fifty or so people – let alone a few thousand – they cannot all still have contact with and relate to the customers. A structure is devised in which they can work efficiently and departments are formed, all of which are responsible for part of the customer services. Each department is then steered in terms of that chunk of service for which they are responsible. Marketing sets out to achieve a good brand perception and retain customers,

Sales aims to attract new customers, the Contact Center must handle contact moments as effectively as possible, the Back Office must ensure that all communication sent to the customer is correct, Online is responsible for a good website, et cetera et cetera.

The greater the number of departments, the greater their detachment from the customer. In many large organizations, direct contact with customers eventually lies solely in the hands of the customer service employees. No wonder then that the organization's customer centricity requires attention across the board. By examining the service you provide throughout the chain from the customer's perspective, every person playing a role in this chain becomes aware of his or her impact on the customer. And so you can re-engage the customer.

Conflicting targets

The various departments not only have insight limited to part of the customer services, but often also have conflicting interests. The purpose of the marketing department is to retain customers, and attracting appropriate customers with the right customer value is crucial to their success. The sales department aims to reel in as many new customers as possible, and customer value is irrelevant. Sales will tempt customers with short-term financial benefits, such as discounts. A year later, these are precisely the customers who will go off bargain hunting for their next best deal. It is therefore important to find the right balance between effectively managing a department and contributing towards mutual goals throughout the customer journey.

Cooperation is paramount to corporate structure

More and more organizations seek the solution to this problem in the design of a matrix organization: chain managers or customer process managers are appointed alongside the departments, and are responsible for customer services throughout the chain. While this may seem extremely logical, it is often found to be counterproductive in practice. At the end of the day, the chain or process managers have less mandate than the responsible departmental managers, resulting in the departmental interests overruling those of the chain. Any reorganization starts with someone drawing the rake shape (the organizational chart).

Yet in day-to-day business, the corporate structure is found to be largely insignificant when it comes to achieving goals over the end-to-end customer journey. Much more important is the intention to cooperate. If the corporate structure facilitates full chain cooperation but those involved are not willing to work together, then it is not going to happen. Conversely, this is easily accomplished in an organization without a formal chain structure but with a willingness to help each other improve the customer's experience. It is vital to pay attention to the degree of cooperation and to the underlying reasons why this does not occur. After all, a customer-centric organization must cooperate over the entire chain, as customers simply do not think in terms of departments, but instead experience the services provided throughout the chain.

1.2 The added value of customer centricity

As an organization grows – and naturally becomes more complex – it is easy to lose sight of customers. But is that really a problem? In other words, is there really any point to focusing on customers, or can organizations survive quite nicely without continuously tuning their services to customers' needs? There are at least four proven benefits of greater customer centricity in organizations.

1. Better competitive position

Over the past twenty to thirty years, organizations have been increasingly faced with competition. Simply supplying a good product at a fair price no longer suffices. This can be simply copied after all. The arrival of Internet has certainly played a role in increasing the competition even further. Nowadays, your unique selling point (USP) is more likely to be found in the service enjoyed by customers. Back in the year 2000, Gilmore and Pine's book *The Experience Economy* described the importance of customer experience, suggesting that the organization is a theater, in which customers seek such an experience. Their vision is exaggerated. Of course it applies to parties such as Disneyland, which many organizations like to visit as a source of inspiration for their own customer centricity. However, customers looking to take out insurance are hardly likely to want an insurance agent to put on such a theatrical experience.

The same applies to anyone looking for a new job, when informing the local council of a house move or querying an Internet subscription. Customer centricity is most certainly crucial for sustained competitive advantage, but as this book will explain, it often lies in unexpected areas.

2. Increased profitability

What has also become more and more clear over the past 20 years is that customer centricity is profitable. In the early days, it took great effort to convince organizations of the importance of focusing on customers, as they were convinced that it was an expensive business. However, from the 1990s on, many studies have been undertaken and books written, giving firm evidence for the fact that organizations with loyal customers and loyal employees are much more profitable than their counterparts where this is not the case (including Reichheld, 1996; Heskett and Sasser, 1997; Fornell, 2007). The service profit chain (Heskett and Sasser, 1997) clearly demonstrates the relationship between the loyalty of employees, quality of services, customer loyalty and profitability (see figure 1.1). Unfortunately, the fact that these books exist is no guarantee that everyone will read them. There was still plenty of missionary work to be done in that field. In the end, the arrival of the Net Promoter Score (Reichheld, 2003) had great impact in demonstrating the importance of loyalty and its relationship to profitability. While copious information is available about the NPS (see also chapter 4), one of the most important aspects of the introduction of the NPS has indeed proven to be: rendering the profitability of loyal customers and thereby customer experience visible right up to the board level. In 2017 even McKinsey has published results that organizations in general see a 5-10% increase in turnover within 2-3 years*.

---

* http://www.mckinsey.com/business-functions/digital-mckinsey/our-insights/putting-customer-experience-at-the-heart-of-next-generation-operating-models

3. Increased cost efficiency

A less well-known yet equally valuable benefit can be found in terms of cost efficiency. This can be particularly profitable in large organizations with a great volume of customer contact, by continuously improving services from the customer point of view. In individual cases, a telecom organization, energy supplier and insurance company eliminated 20 to 40 percent of unnecessary customer contact, resulting in a better customer experience. They were able to do so by identifying reasons for customers seeking contact, analyzing weaknesses in the end-to-end customer journey and then improving them. Depending on the scope of the organization, such reductions can soon translate into cost savings or leeway for investment of as much as a few million dollars (see chapter 5). In the same study as mentioned above on the increase of turnover, McKinsey finds an overall cost reduction of 25-30% in 2-3 years through customer experience.

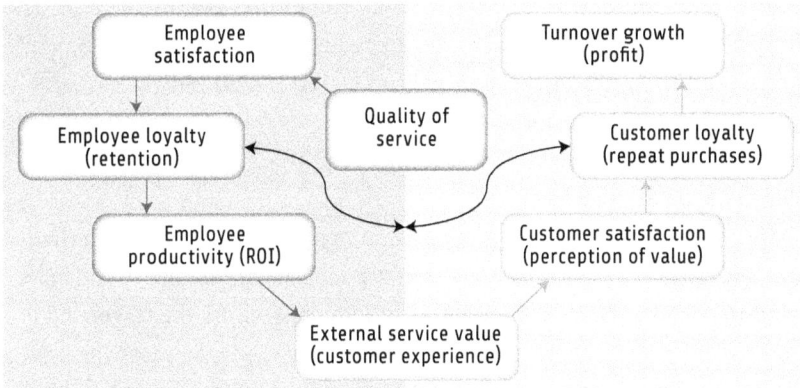

Figure 1.1 *The relationship between customers, employees and profitability (Heskett and Sasser, 1997)*

4. Visibility of good service

The most recently recognized benefit which is increasingly cited, is the transparency of the quality of the service. Thanks to the Internet, we can all announce our experiences to the world – whether positive or negative. And although this is often argued to be the reason for organizations suffering due to their lack of customer centricity, we must question whether this is actually true. Dell was certainly bothered by

Jeff Jarvis' 2005 blog, while United Airlines missed out on sales after a singer in a band composed a song to address the fact that United had broken his guitar, which was seen by 15 million people on You-Tube*. Yet Dell is still a very successful company and United Airlines remains one of the largest airlines in America. So how much does it actually hurt if customers make scathing remarks about you? And conversely of course: just how much benefit is gained from positive publicity? Those people who are intrinsically convinced of the importance of customer centricity can now be heard thinking: "Surely that's not what it's all about? You just want to offer customers good service, and isn't it great if they react positively?" Very true indeed. However, there are virtually no organizations employing only people with such intrinsic conviction. Thus energy needs to be invested in demonstrating that customer centricity yields results. Within a context in which choices are preferably made on the basis of facts and figures – coupled to financial impact where possible – such transparency of service is often tricky when looking to convince the entire organization of the importance of improved customer experience. The first three benefits mentioned then tend to be more effective on the whole.

Sights are set very low

More and more organizations can be heard to bemoan the fact that consumers and citizens are becoming increasingly demanding. That more and more effort is required to exceed expectations in order to score the targeted 8 or more in terms of customer satisfaction. But is that really the case? There are so many gains yet to be made – read: expectations to be exceeded – by first doing the groundwork. It may not be sexy, but it is the reality. In a survey (Van der Aa, 2011) on exceeding expectations, the question was posed: when was your expectation exceeded and why? The answers included: "That they reacted at all." How many people are not genuinely surprised and delighted when an organization actually keeps to their promise to return a call within 24 hours?

You can dispute the claim that customers are increasingly demanding. The claim that expectations have never been so low, is more realistic. As an example of the demanding nature of customers, an organization stated that they required a status update of a request nowadays. Is that so demanding? Surely it should be a standard service? The customer is not even requiring the process to be speeded up, but simply wishes to be kept informed of the progress. The fact that this is a complex process due to the speed of today's technological developments, resulting in customers wanting to receive a WhatsApp message rather than an e-mail, is an entirely different matter. The same applies to complicated legacy systems in the back office, which cannot be simply updated to provide easy-access website tracking and tracing for customers. And so the claim goes much further: the context of the organization and particularly the speed of technological developments makes it increasingly difficult to meet the customers' not so rapidly changing needs. (Haven't we always appreciated being kept informed of progress when something takes a long time?)

1.3 The added value of customer signals management

Ask people for an example of an organization which performs well in terms of customer experience, and they will not readily produce a name. It is easier to name examples where things went wrong, when an agreement was not kept or a company could not be contacted. After all, this is more likely to happen to people, than them being pleasantly surprised by an organization. That is interesting, when considering that organizations have recognized the need for customer centricity for many years. It is very telling in terms of the complexity of customer centricity in larger organizations, and requires methods with an eye for such complexity. What makes customer signals management such a usable method in putting customer centricity into practice within such a complex context? It is a combination of three elements which makes the difference.

1. Measurability
Loyalty and social media share a common drawback when used as a crowbar in the transition to increased customer centricity. It is impossible to calculate the short-term financial consequences for either, without making assumptions. While impact calculations are made via social media, they are by their very nature full of assumptions. After

all, very few organizations can know which social media accounts their own customers use, in order to monitor the actual effect of the social media behavior in terms of matters such as declining sales or even loss of customers.

While customer value and loyalty can certainly be calculated, you cannot be sure whether your estimate has actually become reality until the longer term. An organization can easily see whether or not a person is still their customer a month later, despite a disappointing service experience. Even if he is indeed still around a month later, what will be the effect of that disappointing experience on the customer's loyalty and value in years to come? We therefore require other methods to prove the value of customer centricity for your organization, with the fewest possible assumptions and in the shortest possible time. Customer signals management offers a solution: identifying the most impactful investment in customer satisfaction while reducing costs by improving service from the customer's perspective.

2. Simplicity

Divisions, departments, processes, channels, products, services, procedures, (personal) interests, working instructions, performance indicators... An organization is a complex phenomenon. That internal complexity will trip you up, if you're not careful. It is often the point at which new initiatives flounder, when losing sight of the wood for the trees. The great advantage of customer signals management is that it is always based on the customer's perspective. While a process chart may appear extremely complex, a description of the end-to-end customer journey (which steps does the customer take when passing through your organization?, see chapter 3) has never proven to be complex. However large the organization – however many products, target groups and departments – it is easily simplified as long as you regard services from the customer's point of view. After all, he or she offers an extremely worthwhile and objective perspective which transcends all kinds of personal and departmental interests.

3. Flexibility

The customer signals approach comprises a set of various elements, which can be combined to be optimally geared to the organization wishing to apply customer signals management, depending on the context of the organization. If an organization wishes to reduce costs for example, the first step is to analyze any unnecessary customer contact. And if an organization is looking to create extremely loyal customers, it must first determine which knobs must be turned to score 8 or higher for customer satisfaction. Has the organization worked with autonomous teams for many years? Facilitate these teams with the new insight, and they can continue with their business. In the case of a production-centric organization (a category which also includes many service companies, where departments work through x number of cases per day), you'll require extra focus on the hierarchy, and employees will need much more intensive steering to work with the newfound insight. It is a question of identifying the possibilities available to you and opting for those elements of the approach which are most valuable at the current time.

TIPS & TOOLS

Share perspectives

Not everyone within the organization will immediately share the aspiration to increase customer centricity. The management may be satisfied with the customer focus, while employees are not. Or the management believes there is a need for greater customer focus in the organization while employees feel they are working hard, day in day out, to help customers where possible. They lack a mutual language to describe the nature of their customer-centric organization, and definition of where the parties believe the organization now stands.

Table 1.1 distinguishes between the characteristics of a production-centric organization, a customer-centric organization and a people-centric organization. In daily practice, the classification is never as black and white, but it is a useful tool to encourage the various parties to discuss their ideas.

	Production-centric	Customer-centric	People-centric
Vision	Eye for the product	Eye for the customer	Eye for the person: customer and employee
Management style	Directive, top-down	Well-defined responsibilities	Autonomous responsibility, bottom-up
Vision of operating results	Profit is primary	Customer centricity boosts profit	People centricity is primary, profit is a logical consequence
Cooperation	All parties perform their own tasks	Cooperation within the department	Cooperation between the departments
Vision of employee role	Passive performance by employees	Tasks performed to help the customer	Active input by employees
Commitment by employees	Commitment to their own task	Commitment to customers	Commitment to entire organization
Retention of employees	Too low or too high	Average	High
Reaction to developments	Reactive	Proactive to customers, reactive to employees	Proactive
Organizational development	Conservative	Innovative front office, conservative back office	Innovative
Customer retention	Low	Average/high	High

1.4 The four spearheads of customer signals management

A change of tack towards greater customer centricity affects the organization as a whole. Likewise, customer signals management influences the entire organization. The four spearheads of customer signals management have been designed to help you have an eye for all aspects. They are: customers, employees, continuous improvement and the organization system.

1. Customers

Whatever you do with customer signals management, revolves around the customer. You quite literally bring the customer into the organization. You do so by making use of the customer journey, by knowing exactly which knobs to turn to enhance customer satisfaction (see chapter 4), by analyzing customer contact moments (see chapter 5), by entering into a dialog with customers, by assessing their beliefs, et cetera. You provide a continuous mirror held up by the customer, to increase the organization's awareness of what it means to actually think and work from the customer's perspective.

2. Employees

Every transaction undertaken by a customer involves an employee. The most obvious customer contact moments are those in which customers have direct contact with employees, when calling, mailing and chatting. However, organizations are much less aware of the role of all employees 'without customer contact'. The invoicing department letter was written by an employee. The online application form and confirmation which subsequently lands in my inbox, were designed by an employee. The packaging of my product was produced by an employee. You therefore need to take employee roles into account in all aspects of customer signals management (see chapter 8). Once they have become aware of the importance of their own role from the customer's perspective, seven-league boots may be donned.

3. Continuous improvement

All organizations want to keep improving their services, creating an atmosphere in which employees proactively tackle any issues which can be done better; in which the organization is not afraid to experiment, and instead applies experiments to check the effect of an improvement – with direct adjustment if necessary and a roll-out if the experiment is a success. Working on the basis of this spearhead, we can consistently check what is needed for continuous improvement and can discover any obstacles currently in the way (see also chapter 7).

4. Organization system

After working together for a while, mechanisms will always be formed within the organization system. Mechanisms of which there is no internal awareness, because they are so self evident. Do we address each others' responsibilities? Is our behavior exemplary? But also: to what extent is the required customer centricity and continuous improvement embedded in our performance and assessment cycle? What are the KPIs of the various directors and managers, and are they mutually sustaining or antagonistic? In other words, to what degree can our organization systems facilitate the required shift towards enhanced customer centricity?

TIPS & TOOLS

Use of the four spearheads in practice

A certain division of a public sector organization feels the need to develop into a more customer-centric organization. An initiative has recently been taken to change the working approach throughout the organization, from focusing on systems to focusing on people, based on five themes which represent the required transition.

These are always tricky processes, being abstract, poorly tangible and difficult to concretize. You want the development to be implemented in manageable bites, without having a three-year plan cast in stone. You need the flexibility to react to situations and to take the most effective next step towards that dot on the horizon. Often lacking is the big picture, from which all parties understand what is going on and in which the activities are mutually supportive and supplementary.

The four spearheads of customer signals management have proven to be a great tool for initiating the required development within the organization. Concrete activities can be identified per spearhead, and then divided over year one, for example. The next step is to introduce the process to all involved: from discussing the specific meaning of customer centricity and the themes for working methods, and including this in the HR cycle, all the way through to actually implementing improvements in the customer services offered.

Customers
In order to judge the customer's perspective, each relevant customer process is subjected to an assessment based on the end-to-end customer journey

(see chapter 3). Everyone then knows exactly which knobs need to be turned to boost customer satisfaction. An overview is shared monthly, giving the satisfaction score for these processes, along with a customer's story based on the assessment, a complaint or some other signal. Such clear customer satisfaction steering information allows the MT to be called to account for the (lack of) measurable results from the customer's perspective, regarding those chain processes for which they are responsible.

Employees

Sessions are planned with the employees in order to discuss how the themes apply to them. How can we call each other to account? What are we actually saying if we find errors to be acceptable? Once there is clarity on the behavior required by this working method, each theme is rendered current in six-week cycles. What effective examples of theme X have you encountered this week? What is holding us back in theme X? Employees present the role played by theme X within the organization, based on customer cases, and are allowed to provide feedback to managers, on how theme X is implemented by their MT.

Continuous improvement

Many organizations already have some form of Lean program, which combines well with continuous improvement based on customer input. This continuous improvement is often only visible to those directly involved. If the 'continuous improvement virus' is to be disseminated throughout the organization, it will require additional attention. Once a month, share an attractive example of an improvement achieved by one of the teams, which had tangible results for the customer. This links customers, employees and the continuous improvement process.

Organization system

Perhaps one of the most important components of the customer signals management process is exemplary behavior. If errors are permissible, make sure you share the errors made as a manager, with your people. Each month, show how all managers call a customer who has complained, for example, and then discuss the experience gained in that call. Each manager must perform 'a day in the life of' in a position outside of his own department, but in the chain to which he belongs. This part of the process also includes embedding the new way of working in the HR cycle. How will we assess customer centricity? And what action should be taken if people continually fail to score well for this theme? Will we persevere and prove that we stand behind the movement we have initiated? This spearhead also allows you to consider the way in which you will monitor the transition. Is there a positive development in the identified themes, when assessed every three months? What is successful? And what not? Where is the discrepancy between the two, and what can you learn from this in order to continually and dynamically gear the transition process to the requirements of the moment?

The four spearheads approach helps you devise no end of examples of specific activities to be tackled, in which you can interconnect the four spearheads to make them mutually reinforcing, rather than simply dealing with individual components.

Simple, small, speedy and start tomorrow

Such themes directly touch on the change management discipline, without attention for which it is impossible to actually move the entire organization one step forward. Yes, this is indeed part of customer signals management but at the same time is not the core of the approach. The strength of customer signals management lies in the balance between recognizing the bigger picture based on the four spearheads and always pragmatically initiating a minor detail: a customer process, a satisfaction survey, a customer signals management scan. If you jump into the big picture straightaway, you will lose people. By keeping it small – simple, immediately applicable – you create enthusiasm and establish the foundation for spreading the customer signals management oil stain. At the same time, it is always useful to work from a chain and to determine which elements from neighboring disciplines, such as change management and continuous improvement, can contribute to the successful implementation of customer signals management.

The following chapter explains the precise meaning of customer signals management. What is a signal? What sources of signals can be identified? What are the ten steps of the customer signals management process?

2 WHAT IS CUSTOMER SIGNALS MANAGEMENT?

The best way to get to know yourself is to try to understand others

— ANDRÉ GIDE

Customer signals management came into being as the (r)evolution of complaints management. It is a method by which you continuously improve your services, based on all the signals received from customers and resulting in a better customer experience and measurable results in terms of both customer satisfaction and cost reduction.

2.1 The crux of customer signals management

It has proven difficult to actually improve customer services in the case of complaints management, as this soon becomes a discussion about the number of complaints, which is relatively low versus the number of customers or number of customer contacts. The result is often less than 1 percent. The race for capacity and budget is lost before it is even run. As we all know, the actual number of complaints is considerably higher than the number of registered complaints. Some studies have shown that for every complaint submitted, 26 customers with the same complaint did not bother to submit it (Barlow and Moller, 1996). Despite the commonly quoted definition of complaints as 'any expression of discontent', many complaints are not registered as such. But if that can't be proven, you will have a tough time claiming that the improvement of customer experience based on complaints can be extremely profitable for the organization.

Make customer experience steerable

So how can you push customer experience up the priority list? By speaking the organization's language, by making customer experience steerable. Customer signals management allows you to draw together all signals and add a price tag. As every organization also has a financial drive, this method of rendering customer experience measurable can be used to create mass, and thereby priority. The customer experience is rendered steerable not only by translating avoidable customer contact moments into money, but also by designing your customer satisfaction survey to give precise answers regarding the most profitable investment. Many organizations already conduct customer satisfaction surveys, without having any idea what should actually be improved. "Should I boost that 6 for waiting time to a 7, or is it smarter to get that 7 for turnaround time up to an 8, to improve customers' rating of my application procedure?"

Chapter 4 teaches you how to design your customer satisfaction survey to answer this question for the organization.

Beyond intentions

Of course each organization has the intrinsic drive to do right by the customer, to use every complaint as a source for improvement. Such an intention will be found at virtually all companies. And there lies the greatest risk: that it remains an intention. The same organizations are faced with the cold, harsh reality that very little can actually be done in terms of improvement and change unless that required improvement can be justified in hard cash. However much they would like to change the situation, the reality is that the financial drive has priority. Customer signals management takes advantage of this: you translate your required results into a financial picture. People understand that and can weigh it more effectively than when translating it in terms of experience.

Measurable customer experience at work

An organization receives one hundred complaints annually about the 100,000 invoices which are sent. The cost of processing each complaint is 50 dollars.

The total annual cost of the complaints is therefore 100 × 50 dollars = 5000 dollars. This is peanuts for most organizations, which are therefore unlikely to free capacity to improve customer service on this point. Rightly so. After all, most of your customers are not complaining, so just how representative are those complaints for the general customer experience of your service?

The same organization also receives 5000 e-mails and 15,000 telephone calls about the invoices, on top of the one hundred complaints. An e-mail costs 15 dollars to process and a telephone call 10 dollars. Suddenly, the total costs of customer contact regarding invoices have risen from 5000 dollars to 230,000 dollars. Now that is a serious amount. The priority has now been created to improve the customer service in invoicing. By combining the various types of customer contact, instead of simply counting complaints, you create a much broader basis for identification of where things are going wrong, in the customers' opinion.

When also linking this to the satisfaction survey, you can connect all types of signals and determine the priority very precisely. Most of the aforementioned customer contact moments concern questions about unclear amounts on invoices. The customer satisfaction survey on the invoicing process, and the subsequent model analysis of the survey (see chapter 4) showed that, from the customer's point of view, clarity had three times more impact on satisfaction, than simply speeding up the invoice turnaround time.

The person responsible for invoicing now knows how to significantly boost customer satisfaction while at the same time saving 230,000 dollars, by improving the clarity of his invoices.

Customer signals management almost always provides a win-win situation: you tackle the points for improvement which increase customer satisfaction ("I just don't want to have to call about an unclear invoice") and simultaneously save costs (less unnecessary contact moments and therefore lower processing costs).

2.2 The definition of a signal

Customer signals management is based on drawing together the appropriate signals from customers and sharing the signals throughout the organization, so that each department can tackle their own improvement points. The organization can be mobilized, by linking the customer experience activities to measurable results in terms of costs and customer satisfaction.

But when is something a signal? And do we really need to define a signal? The latter has been proven necessary in practice. An organization received a signal from an employee that there was a new stapler on the market, which produced much finer staples than those currently used. An excellent idea indeed, which could easily be realized within the department, but it is not a customer signal.

More and more organizations seem to think that every contact moment is a signal. This is not only an incorrect definition but also one which is not viable in practice. Most organizations have so many sources of signals that it is impossible to take action for every contact moment, every comment in a customer satisfaction survey, et cetera. Your organization would drown in a sea of signals, with no sign of a lifebuoy. Capacity and budget are limited after all, and so you need only tackle signals that matter.

Basically, a signal is a sign that something requires structural improvement, but not every contact is a reason for such improvement. There are three axes by which you can determine whether a contact is a signal (see table 2.1).

No signal	Signal
Incident	Point for improvement
Deal with contact	Improve due to contact
Desirable contact	Undesirable contact

Table 2.1 *When is something a signal?*

1. Incident versus point for improvement

Customer signals management must not be confused with incident management. As soon as a website is down, an organization has a process with which the incident can be solved as quickly as possible and the website relaunched. Once the incident re-occurs more frequently, the time has come to acknowledge this as being a signal. Something is structurally wrong, in this case the website.

2. Deal with a contact or learn from a contact?

The process of dealing with a contact moment (telephone call, e-mail, etc.) is not the same as the process of learning from that contact moment. These are two totally separate things, which also require different competences and processes. Take the difference between dealing with a complaint and learning from a complaint, for example. The goal when dealing with a complaint is to solve the problem perceived by the complainant. It is an individual case, requiring a solution for the complaint, preferably one which satisfies the customer. The goal when learning from complaints is to prevent any further complaints about that specific subject. In this case, you analyze the cause of the complaint in order to solve it and to avoid other customers suffering the same inconvenience.

3. Desirable contact versus undesirable contact

Some processes are designed in order to invite contact. Think in terms of the cancellation process: organizations often want customers to seek telephone contact. This contact moment is not a signal that your cancellation process requires improvement. If on the other hand, customers call to inquire about the status of their cancellation, that is a signal that this point in the process can be improved (made shorter or better information provided for customers). Some contact points can be valuable for commercial organizations. They may offer good sales opportunities, because there is maximum relevance for the customer at that moment in time. Complex issues in the public sector are sometimes better solved by telephone or in person, as they may otherwise require multiple e-mails and phone calls back and forth. Once again there are shades of gray: not all contact moments are necessarily undesirable.

2.3 Sources of signals

There are many sources from which signals can be derived, and the range of signals is immense. Any form of customer contact from which you can derive input, is a source of signals. A (non exhaustive) list of possible sources is given below.

1. Telephone calls

While you can derive signals from telephone calls, not every telephone call is necessarily a signal. Regularly occurring telephone calls are a sign that something is structurally wrong. Telephone calls that are simply part of the process on the other hand, are not a signal. You may wish customers to call your organization at impactful moments (such as divorce or death) for example, in order that you can react with maximum empathy. These are not signals that the process itself requires improvement. A useful starting point is to generate a top-10 list of call subjects. Chapter 5 tells you more about useful contact registration in order to recognize the appropriate signals.

2. E-mail, chat, WhatsApp

These signals are governed by the same rules as telephone calls, though there is the great advantage of them being written texts. You therefore have many more tools at your fingertips to classify their contents into the most commonly occurring subjects and the appropriate signals. Most e-mail and web care packages can be linked to reporting tools such as Business Objects, which allow you to simply define characteristics for statistical purposes. For example: count the number of messages which include 'cancel' in the subject or text. The challenge in this case is to choose exactly those terms used by customers, to achieve an accurate tally. For a cancellation, you may need to count the following words: cancel, cancellation, terminate, termination, leaving, et cetera.

3. Web care

This channel also offers the advantage of providing written text, with a multitude of tools available to analyze this information. The disadvantage is that all the messages are extremely brief. There is a good chance therefore that extra work will be required to identify the real signals concealed within the messages.

4. Complaints

The registration of complaints requires the same degree of caution as the registration of telephone calls. You must be able to periodically analyze complaints in order to discover the signals for structural points for improvement. Take extra care here not to make the registration so general that you really have no idea where the signals may be found. Categories such as 'information and communication' are no exception at many companies! When defining registration categories, always think in terms of: "Do I know where to start when using this for improvement?"

5. Customer panel

Generally speaking, there are two types of customer panels: a live panel, in which you deal with a subject in depth with ten customers, face-to-face for example, and an online panel, with which you can ask up to 20,000 or 30,000 people about all kinds of subjects. A panel is always useful when looking for in-depth knowledge. It is therefore a great tool when identifying the cause of signals, but not useful as a source with which to reel in the net of signals.

6. NPS studies

There are many different types of Net Promoter Score (NPS) studies by now, though they are all still based on the NPS question itself, followed by the 'why' question: "Would you recommend us?" followed by the open question: "Why would you (not) recommend us?" This is a rich source of signals, due to it being an open question concerning an extremely broad evaluation (recommendation). At the same time, that is precisely the disadvantage of this method. It is often so general that it proves tricky to identify specific, useful signals. Chapter 4 gives an overview of the pros and cons of the NPS versus CSAT (Customer Satisfaction) versus CES (Customer Effort Score).

7. Customer satisfaction survey

There are many variants of this type of survey by now: from the shortest version with a single question featuring smileys or stars to the most extensive questionnaires for model analyses (see chapter 4). Just like all other signals, the advice once again is: be careful which one you use. If you wish to know which knobs to turn to gage satisfaction with the customer introduction process, the single question/smiley option will not suffice. That same single question may well be fine if you only want to check the thermometer for a very specific improvement prompted by an earlier signal.

It probably goes without saying, but once again: stay realistic about what is feasible. If you are just starting, use the sources already at your disposal rather than tapping into all kinds of new sources. The organization must also be able to cope with the input. And successfully engaging the improvement process (see also chapter 7) is much more complex than simply gathering more signals and performing analyses.

TIPS & TOOLS

Direct individual versus structurally improved customer experience

The primary focus of customer signals management lies in customer experience for all customers, and the scope of most organizations forces you to evaluate this. However, there are opportunities at the individual level, in which you can deploy customer signals management to exceed individual customers' expectations. By calling all customers who complain, for example, by actively approaching all customers who score below a certain level for customer satisfaction, or by proactively returning calls to all customers who call often, to check whether you can help them. All kinds of tools are available nowadays to organize this simply using business rules.

This really works wonders for the individual customer perception, as became apparent in an organization which proactively returned the calls of the 10 most regularly calling customers in that month (so-called frequent callers). The customers scored this initiative with nines and tens. The ultimate customer experience! When studying the causes of this frequent contact and what they could learn from it, the employees could not detect any signals other than those already derived from the available reports.

You therefore need to choose where to focus your energy. Are you looking to achieve a positive direct and individual experience? Then proactively seek individual contact based on signals. Do you want structural improvements? There's no need to individually call your customers to discover what has gone wrong, but rather focus your energy on undertaking the appropriate improvements.

2.4 The position of customer signals management within the organization

There are all kinds of signals to be gathered, but how can you ensure that they give you effective insight? Generally speaking, each department tends to gather its own signals. The complaints department makes complaints analyses, the marketing department conducts research, the contact center registers telephone calls, et cetera. They all then converge on the responsible department, each with their own top-10 list. And so the invoicing department is visited by someone from complaints on Monday, receives the results of the satisfaction survey on Wednesday and is provided with the most frequently asked questions about the invoice, by the contact center, a week later. This all makes it disorderly for the responsible department, giving the process a very 'ad hoc' feeling. What is really the problem? Where lies the true profit? What focus is required over the next three months? These are the questions you need to answer for the responsible managers. In doing so, you help the people necessary for improving customer satisfaction with their own objectives, and together you book results.

You need to centrally gather, group and analyze all the signals (see figure 2.1). They can then be shared with the persons responsible for tackling the signals. They are the internal customers. The invoicing department manager is only fed signals relevant to him, rather than signals in which he plays no role. This creates focus and urgency. Forget all the separate top-10 lists, concentrate instead on an integral map giving the location of the sore points.

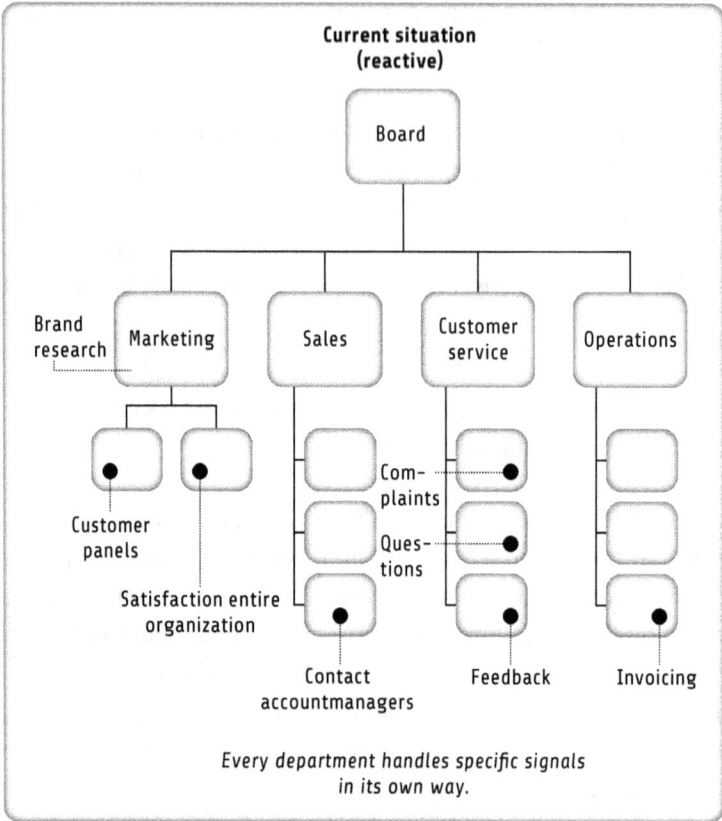

Figure 2.1 *The position of customer signals management within the organization*

The customer signals management scan

Once you are enthusiastic about customer signals management, it is often useful to start with a customer signals management scan. A common denominator seen in virtually all organizations is that the various signals are recorded in very different ways. Complaints registration uses completely different categories to telephony registration. And the customer satisfaction survey evaluates themes very unlike the categories used for registration of complaints and telephony. A water company, for example, included the yearly bill as a complaints category, while it was not found anywhere in the telephony and satisfaction survey records.

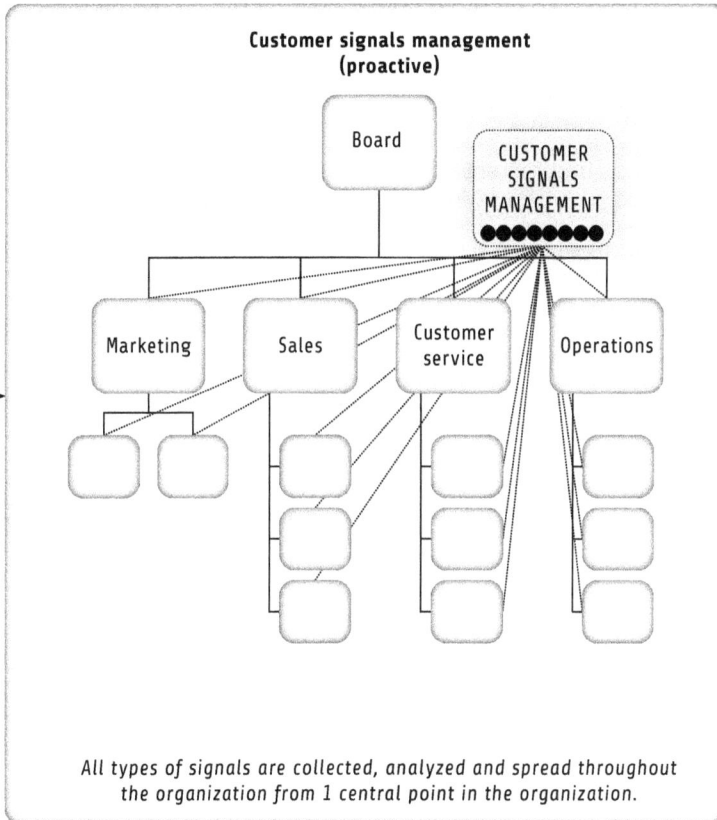

Customer signals management (proactive)

All types of signals are collected, analyzed and spread throughout the organization from 1 central point in the organization.

Figure 2.1 *The position of customer signals management within the organization (cont.)*

As customer signals management relies on the symbiosis of all the signals, this is an extremely important interim step. For each type of signal available to you, ascertain how registration currently takes place. Now analyze where the registration converges and where it diverges. First check whether you can manually bring the various categories together in order to get started (invoice and invoicing go well together for example). Next, determine how the registration systems can be adapted to automatically bring the categories together in the future.

The location of the customer signals management role or department is unimportant. Figure 2.1 shows it alongside the board, but it may not be necessary at that level. Much more important is that the person responsible for bringing customer signals management to life in the organization must be informally popular, be proficient in his or her subject matter, be sensitive and full of energy, rather than this person having the correct 'rake' (see chapter 9 for more success factors for customer signals management). Another crucial element in mobilizing your organization is the way in which you present matters. Imagine you are your internal customer. Draw up a very simple and brief report in which this customer exactly identifies the sore points and priorities. Don't fall into the trap of wanting to share all insights and demonstrate all interesting analyses. You need to be relevant and to the point.

2.5 The ten steps of the customer signals management process

When starting to learn from individual signals within an organization, you soon notice the need for a structured process: from gathering signals all the way through to measuring the results of the improvements made. Although there are all kinds of work flow and complaints tools on the market which entail a complete process, they do not facilitate the customer signals management process adequately. We have therefore worked out the customer signals management process into ten concrete steps. These steps may take only an hour for some signals, while others will require a year of your time. Some simple signals do not require impact analysis for example, though you need to record why it was not necessary, in that step. The steps are not intended as a rigid process flow through which each signal must be pressed, but rather a practical tool for transparent steering of the customer signals management process. The ten steps are explained in brief below.

1. Submitting the signal
In the same way as for contact registration, in submitting the signal, you need to find the balance between the ease of submittal and communication of the correct signal characteristics. Does the signal concern a particular channel, a particular customer process or a particular customer group? Think carefully therefore about the infor-

mation required from the signal in order to lend direction to your improvements and to determine which reporting cross sections you wish to use.

Who may submit it?

If you are only just initiating the customer signals management process, it is sensible to limit the number of employees who are allowed to submit signals. Start with one person per department, for example, and learn how the process works as you go along. It can then be expanded when appropriate.

2. Reviewing the signal

In the early days in particular, there will not always be clarity on whether or not something is a signal. This step is therefore very relevant. It entails nothing more than checking whether the submitted signal is covered by the definition and whether you understand it. This is not the time for a contextual check or any form of impact analysis, which will follow later on. It is quite simply a brief check of the signal itself.

3. Impact analysis

This step concerns the significance of rendering the signal measurable, requiring you to combine all the signals. This is where you determine the magnitude of an individual signal. You do so along two axes: customer satisfaction and customer contacts.

Impact of customer satisfaction

Based on the model analyses undertaken in your customer satisfaction survey (see chapter 4), you are familiar with the important aspects for customer satisfaction. Imagine that empathy is the most important factor, and waiting times the least important factor. A signal which relates to empathy will have greater priority than one which relates to the waiting times. You turn your customer satisfaction knobs in order to prioritize which signals count most.

Impact of customer contacts

Based on the contact registration (see chapter 5), you can establish how many contacts have been affected by the submitted signal. Imagine that the submitted signal concerns an ambiguous invoice. At that point, you check how many telephone calls, e-mails, complaints, objections, visits etc. relate to the invoice. These are tallied and multiplied by the costs of processing each contact. You can now calculate the exact costs incurred by this signal and therefore define its significance, both for your customers and for the organization. If there is no calculation of the costs per contact available within the organization, the following benchmark can be applied in order to get a sense of the financial order of magnitude: telephone call 10 dollars, e-mail 15 dollars and a complaint 75 dollars.

Impact on other fronts

There may be other priorities alongside these two axes. Statutory obligations or a tainted image, for example. Determine whether any other axes are relevant for your organization, but try not to make the list of axes too long.

4. Prioritize

After impact analysis, you know whether the signal has great or limited priority from the customer's perspective, namely in terms of satisfaction and customer contact. So why add the prioritize step here? There may always be reasons why a signal defined as high priority in the impact analysis cannot be tackled in the short term. In the example of the invoice, imagine that a project is underway in which the entire invoicing system is to be replaced within the next six months, in order to remove any ambiguity. There is then no point investing a great deal of energy in clarification of the invoice, alongside this project. This signal therefore has no priority for the time being. It can always be given fresh attention once the new system is up and running. In this phase therefore, you look at the internal context relevant to whether or not the customer signal requires action.

5. Analyze the cause

The previous steps provided you with insight into the magnitude of the signal but not yet its cause. What we now know is that the invoice costs 100,000 dollars per year and that customers are dissatisfied with it, but we do not yet know why. In this phase, you work at discovering exactly what has gone wrong (see also chapter 7), by analyzing the detailed customer journey (see chapter 3). This step and the following one can be effectively combined with methods such as Lean, if they are already present within the organization.

6. Formulate points for improvement

Once you know the cause, you can also formulate the right points for improvement. This is the phase of the business case in which you determine the costs of the solution. Thanks to the impact analysis, you already know the benefits, so the next main question is: how much must we invest to solve the problem? And is that amount more or less than the benefits to be achieved? If the organization can save 100,000 dollars due to fewer questions concerning invoices, but it costs 500,000 dollars to adapt the system for clearer invoicing, the payback period will be five years. Is that quick enough or is it too expensive after all?

7. Go/no go decision

In this phase, you conduct an internal context check similar to the prioritization step. Once again, your business case may be positive, while there are still reasons not to undertake action. The opposite can also be true: that the business case is negative, yet there are still reasons to tackle issues.

8. Monitor points for improvement

You can now start to implement the formulated points for improvement. One of the greatest pitfalls in this phase is that you forget to follow its progress, and nothing happens in the end. Make sure you monitor progress therefore, that reports are generated on the progress and that more drastic action can be taken if the improvement process loses focus without good reason being given.

9. Measure the effect

After implementing the points for improvement, you can measure whether the activities have had an effect. This is quite simply a (1st) measurement of the baseline measurement already conducted in the impact analysis phase. You have already taken a look at the satisfaction level and the number of customer contacts. And so you know exactly what measurement is required. Has satisfaction increased? Has the number of customer contacts from the impact analysis decreased? If the number of telephone calls has decreased by 1000 versus the impact analysis, this means that you have saved 10,000 dollars.

10. Feed back results

One of the most commonly heard complaints about internal improvement processes is: "I've told them so many times that…, but I never hear anything more about it." If you want to keep everyone enthusiastic and involved, effect measurement is not the only important factor but also the feeding back of results to those involved. This keeps people motivated to submit new signals and sets the customer signals management process structurally in motion.

2.6 Organization of the customer signals management process

The process of designing these ten steps can be quickly arranged, and a process description soon formulated. However, actual implementation of the process in the organization, with definition of who does what, is often a complex puzzle. It is a new process for most people after all, and many organizations are not yet accustomed to making improvements throughout the end-to-end customer journey.

Existing and new responsibilities

Most of the steps in the customer signals management process can be conducted by employees in existing positions. All employees can be signal submitters, the cause analysis can often be made by someone from the quality department, et cetera. A new coordinating role is also necessary however, in order to monitor the total customer signals management process. This person is responsible for correct reporting of the process progress, monitoring the turnaround times of the various phases and motivating when necessary. Such a role is crucial, especially in the beginning when all is new.

Chain versus customer journey

Due to customer signals management being based on the customer journey, it is essential to also form a team to tackle the points for improvement throughout this chain of internal departments that play a role. The organization may already have customer process managers or chain managers, which are ideal positions from which to embed the signals from step 4: prioritize. Don't forget that these roles may also often be based on an internal chain rather than the actual customer chain (the journey). Someone is in charge of the communication chain for example, and is responsible for all content. From a customer journey perspective however, content is but one element, and the turnaround time of a process or the friendliness of an employee is equally important, for example. Make sure you really do have everyone on board from the customer's perspective.

TIPS & TOOLS

Get off to a running start

You are enthusiastic about the customer signals management process and want to introduce it within the organization. Where should you start? Designing the process is not the difficult part, thanks to the ten steps as your guideline. The challenge lies in bringing together all the right parties who play a role in those ten steps and uncovering any barriers to this cooperation. An effective approach in practice is to organize a number of workshops to cater for a very broad representation of the organization. Anyone and everyone involved in improving customer services on the basis of the customer signals management process, must be represented at these workshops. The size of the group is also essential in order that the oil stain of enthusiasm continues to spread.

During the first workshop, you work through the ten steps together, looking at two aspects:

1. What needs to be done in each step and do we have all the required information at hand?
2. Who is to implement each step and does our organization include such a role?

In the impact analysis for example, you require customer contact data and customer satisfaction data. Is that available or has a system yet to be designed? If not, how can you get started in the meantime? Is there some form of customer journey or customer process team for the required roles, who can tackle the signals from step 4 on? This workshop produces a blueprint and the 'to do list' in order to work effectively through the steps.

In the second workshop, you deal with the conditions required to get this blueprint up and running, in the form of a pilot to begin with. Is there capacity for the new role of customer signals management coordinator? Do we have sufficient support from the rest of the organization to be able to experiment with this way of working?

In order not to become bogged down by all the possible challenges envisaged by participants, and to keep the energy from ebbing away at the end of the session, it is useful to round off by asking: "Are there any issues which will make the proposed way of working impossible?" instead of asking: "Will there be any other issues we'll run into?" Both questions will result in a list of points for attention, but the energy of: "No, not impossible, but they do need attention" is completely different to: "Yes, we have a list of points for attention we'll run into". All the input from these workshops can be used to experiment with the customer signals management process in practice, allowing you to fine tune it along the way to render it smarter.

Timing is everything

Most organizations are only just starting to improve their customer experience. It is therefore not practical to start the process of improving services based on individual signals. Much more effective is to use the end-to-end journey as a framework (see chapter 3) in which you can plot all the available signals. You can then choose the top x areas for improvement in which to take action. As you already know the satisfaction level and number of customer contacts for these top x aspects, you immediately know your ROI. This allows for much better steering, and prevents you from drowning in signals in this phase. In concrete terms, you can implement improvements and demonstrate results, straightaway. Start by clearing out the general rubble therefore, before designing the process by which to learn from individual signals. That process will work perfectly once you have laid the foundations and you continue to use them in learning and improving, based on the signals provided by your customers.

The following chapter discusses the importance of the end-to-end customer journey as a framework for customer signals management, the question of how to define the customer end-to-end journey and how it differs from all other customer journeys.

3 THE END-TO-END CUSTOMER JOURNEY AS A FRAMEWORK

It is costly wisdom that is brought by experience.

— ROBERT ASCHAM

The end-to-end customer journey is vital when examining organizations from the customer's perspective. Which steps does the customer take with the organization? These steps form the basis for customer satisfaction surveys and customer contact analyses – in fact for everything you do to achieve more customer-centric services. It is the structure upon which customer signals management initiatives rest.

3.1 The strength of the customer journey

One of the most important steps undertaken by an organization is to actually consider the customer's point of view. The end-to-end customer journey is a fantastic, simple and extremely strong instrument for this purpose. Most organizations are divided into all kinds of divisions and departments, resulting in them completely losing sight of how the customer experiences the total process. Employees only have insight into that section of the process for which they are responsible (making changes in the system), and have no idea how the journey works before them (customer contact requesting a change) or after them (confirmation of documents, payment of money). Creating this end-to-end customer journey is the first concrete and impactful step in the change process, to actually consider the customer's perspective.

The strength of the end-to-end customer journey

For many years, the number 1 complaint heard by an insurance company concerned surrender of annuity policies. Customers felt that the process was either overly long or could not be achieved at all. The manager responsible for the department believed the complaints to be less important than the efficient running of his operation. What's more, all KPIs were positive and the surrender of the product offered no benefits for the insurance company. There was little urgency to take action therefore.

The project leader in charge of improving services based on complaints, then decided to establish the end-to-end customer journey for the process of surrendering an annuity policy. The journey began with the telephone call from a customer looking to surrender his policy, and ended with him receiving the money in his bank account (see figure 3.1). The internal process was performed by various departments: the customer service, the account manager, the back office, the financial department. Each step in the journey had its own internal service levels for turnaround times, which were all achieved. All was well therefore.

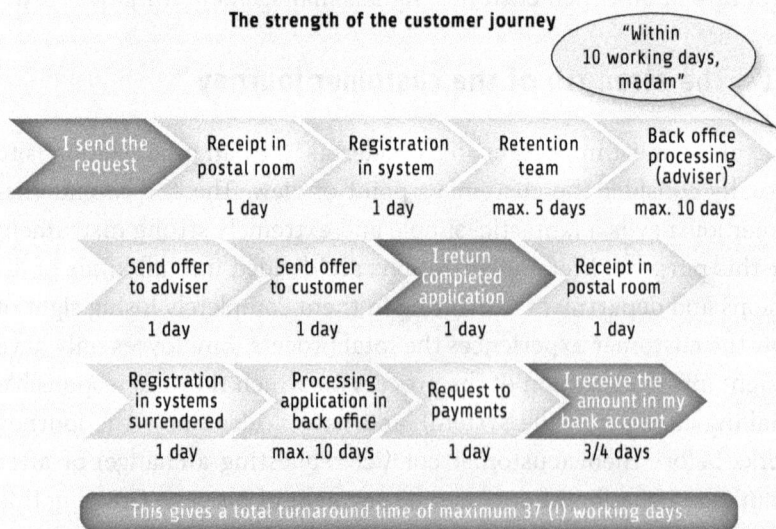

The strength of the customer journey

"Within 10 working days, madam"

I send the request	Receipt in postal room	Registration in system	Retention team	Back office processing (adviser)
	1 day	1 day	max. 5 days	max. 10 days

Send offer to adviser	Send offer to customer	I return completed application	Receipt in postal room
1 day	1 day	1 day	1 day

Registration in systems surrendered	Processing application in back office	Request to payments	I receive the amount in my bank account
1 day	max. 10 days	1 day	3/4 days

This gives a total turnaround time of maximum 37 (!) working days

Figure 3.1 *Customer journey for surrendering an annuity policy*

The dark gray blocks show the steps discernible for the customer. All other steps are internal ones with individual turnaround times. On tallying all the internal turnaround times of the intermediate steps, the total turnaround time was no less than 37 working days. A fact of which the manager was unaware. On calling customer service to ask how long it will take, customers were told: "Your policy will be surrendered within 10 working days." The dark gray steps also show that the customer was left in the dark in the meantime.

Those 37 working days can be a conscious choice, with good reason. You must however keep the customer well informed. After gaining insight into this customer journey, the manager not only saw something completely new to him but also something which could help him boost the efficiency of his operation. A win-win situation which reduced his resistance to complaints and allowed him to tackle the situation together with his department.

Two types of customer journeys

When creating the end-to-end journey, there are two types of journey that play an important role. There are main customer journeys and detailed customer journeys, both of which are necessary and both serve various purposes. The main customer journey displays the general steps taken by the customer within the organization (see figure 3.2).

I become a customer	I pay a premium	I have a question	I enjoy the use of my product	I change my details	I buy another product	I have a complaint	I receive the premium quotation for next year (prolongation)	I terminate one of my products	I terminate the relationship

Figure 3.2 *Example of the main customer journey of an insurance company*

It serves the following purposes:
* a common language and method for customer experience within your organization;
* a clear structure for your signals, which can be plotted per step in this journey;

+ insight into which steps exist and therefore which customer journeys must be detailed per process;
+ initial prioritization of the main customer processes (see also
  chapter 4);
+ insight into each role and its influence on the various steps experienced by the customer.

This main journey is too abstract for any other purposes. If you want
to improve your customers' experience or if you want to reduce costs
within a process, you will need to establish detailed customer journeys for each step in the main journey. Detailed customer journeys
show all steps undertaken by the customer within each customer process (see figure 3.3).

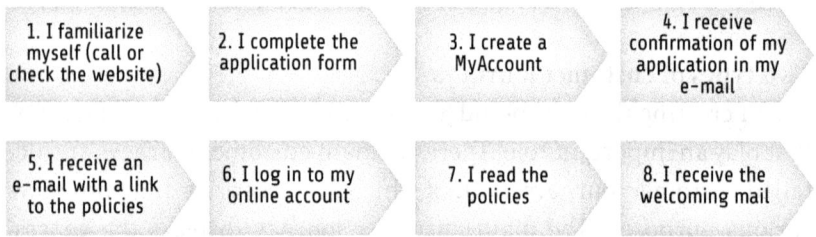

1. I familiarize myself (call or check the website)	2. I complete the application form	3. I create a MyAccount	4. I receive confirmation of my application in my e-mail
5. I receive an e-mail with a link to the policies	6. I log in to my online account	7. I read the policies	8. I receive the welcoming mail

Figure 3.3 *Example of the detailed customer journey 'I become a customer'*

They are used in order to make people aware of their role in the end-
to-end journey, as the basis for determining drivers of customer satisfaction (see also chapter 4) and as the basis for improvement of
services (see also chapter 7).

TIPS & TOOLS

Experience the strength of the detailed journey

A drinking water company wanted its employees to experience for themselves how customers viewed their services. The exercise they undertook in
four groups was to establish the detailed customer journey of another sector, namely that of requesting supplementary benefit. It was based on two

sources: the information given on the website and a Lean value map for the same process. In the plenary discussion of this customer journey, the final step for all four groups was: informing the customer of whether he or she was entitled to receive benefit. Before reading any further, can you imagine which step they all forgot? The actual transfer of money into the customer's account! This is not only a crucial step for the customer but also a relevant step for the organization, which mustn't be omitted. This is an example of how difficult it is to actually think from the end-to-end journey, even when it is not your own process and you are taking a fresh look from outside.

If you want your own organization to experience this, organize a workshop which comprises the following steps:
- Explain the meaning of a detailed customer journey and the usefulness of this method.
- Now have each group:
  - check out the website to find out what customers can read about the process;
  - study any internal process flowcharts;
  - define the detailed customer journey.
- Look and listen. What is conspicuous?
- In the plenary session, concentrate on the process and what the employees notice when looking in this way. Don't be tempted to spend time discussing all the contextual details of the process to be worked out. That can be done at a later stage or in a further workshop. The objective of this phase is to generate awareness of how customers regard services, to collectively think outside of your own box.

3.2 Establishing customer journeys

These journeys are relatively simply formed, though the approach required to establish the main customer journey differs from that for the detailed journey.

Establishing the main journey

The greatest strength of the main customer journey is at the same time the greatest pitfall for its users, namely its simplicity. Looking at services from the customer's perspective, they are nearly always very orderly. When regarding them internally, you can become ensnared in the spaghetti of departments, processes, instructions, exceptions, et cetera. Don't fall into that trap. Always stay well out of the internal discussion and complexity. It's not important in this phase after all. Establishing the main customer journey should take you no longer than an hour, plus a brief round with a number of people involved, to check that you have not omitted important steps.

Establishing the detailed journey

The best way of establishing the detailed customer journey is in a workshop in which you bring together all those involved. When facilitating such sessions, you begin the draft design of the detailed customer journey by checking the steps customers must take in the process, as given on the website. This often not only gives a good understanding but is also an effective homework assignment, as very few people actually look at their own website. Such an intervention helps raise awareness for the outside-in approach.

The right people on board

When defining the people required, it is important to literally invite everyone from the end-to-end journey to participate. What is commonly heard: "yes, we certainly do work with journey teams or customer process teams, so we're already familiar with that composition." But if you persevere and ask whether the team also includes someone from the contact center, website, finance or communications, the answer will be: "No, it doesn't." Be tenacious therefore, to ensure that at least one employee from each of the organization departments which play a role in the customer journey, participates in the workshop. There are no management chairs at this workshop table, but rather those employees responsible for the journey steps on a daily basis.

Asking 'silly' questions

At the start of the workshop, you will almost always encounter people having to introduce themselves to each other because they are meeting for the first time. They have never worked together in this way. During the workshop, you only ask 'silly' questions: What effect will that have on the customer? What do you mean? What's the meaning of that term you just used? Now that you have an initial website-based design, it's time to work through the steps and keep asking what happens there, are there steps missing, and so on until all the steps are complete. You use two mantras during the workshop:

1. *What effect will that have on the customer?* People tend to persist in defining the steps to be taken from the internal organization out, i.e. the internal processes to be followed. In some sessions, they might even discuss internal form codes. That's logical, as they are accustomed to doing so. So keep asking: "Okay, but what effect will that have on the customer?" The only steps to be added to the journey are those which affect the customer.
2. *How often does that happen?* People also tend to name all the exceptions. You must therefore regularly ask how often something happens, whether it is an exception. A useful tool is to ask: "Does it happen in 80 percent of the cases or in 20 percent?" This question will often still be overly abstract for customer service employees. But if you rephrase it: "Is this the case in eight out of ten calls or two out of ten calls?", they're certain to know the answer. The base limit is generally 50 percent. If something happens in more than half of the cases, it should become a step in your journey.

Duration of the steps
Another useful addition is the turnaround time per step. As sketched earlier in 'The strength of the customer journey', very few people are aware of the total turnaround time from the customer's perspective. They each have their own turnaround time target, but when tallying all the individual turnaround times, you will often gain amazing insight.

Initiating the first change
In all their simplicity, these workshops are one of the first real interventions to be made en route to an organization with greater self-awareness from the customer perspective. That is exactly how you should treat the workshops. Take your time, prepare well and make sure they are fun. Virtually all participants will be inspired by this

new mindset and will take that newfound energy back to the rest of the organization.

Examples of other detailed journeys

Because this is such an important tool, here are a number of examples of detailed journeys in the practical situation.

Detailed journey for a chemist – first issue of medication

The reason for establishing this journey (see figure 3.4) is the chemist looking to improve services. Once again, there is often only attention for their own sphere of influence rather than the complete journey. Arrival at the chemist to departure from the chemist therefore. From the chemists' perspective, there is no attention for the GP, nor for the use of the medication once the patient returns home. Yet for customers, the total process of taking new medication encompasses this entire journey. From the customer's perspective therefore, the GP also plays a role in the journey.

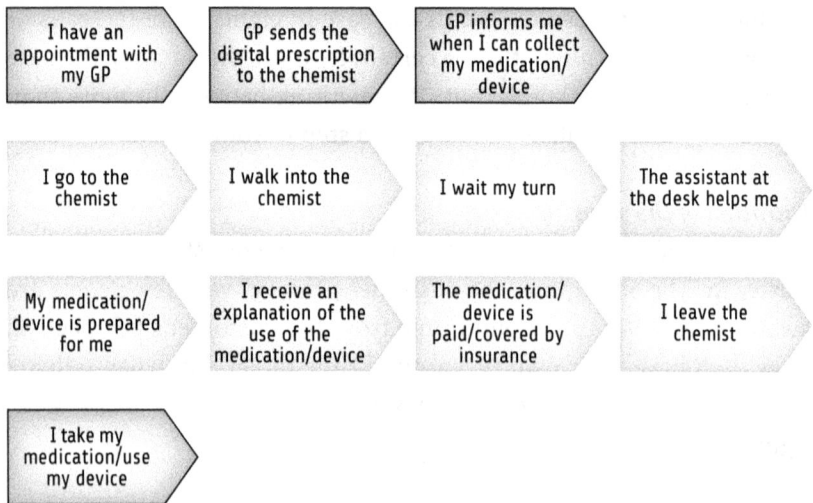

I have an appointment with my GP	GP sends the digital prescription to the chemist	GP informs me when I can collect my medication/ device
I go to the chemist	I walk into the chemist	I wait my turn	The assistant at the desk helps me
My medication/ device is prepared for me	I receive an explanation of the use of the medication/device	The medication/ device is paid/covered by insurance	I leave the chemist
I take my medication/use my device		

Figure 3.4 *Customer journey for first issue of medication*

The same applies to the step in which the patient is informed about whether or not this medication is covered by insurance, which is not always determined by the chemist. The chemist's assistant may well say: "There's nothing I can do about that", but that doesn't really count if you want to improve the customer experience. If the perception of the costs plays a role for the customer, you need to be aware of this in order that you know its impact on customer satisfaction. A great deal can often also be achieved through effective communication. Imagine a situation in which customers are dissatisfied with the GP and this affects the way they assess the first issuing process. The chemist can approach the GP and exercise influence to improve the situation. You therefore have much more influence than you would often believe. To do so, you must however have visualized the total journey and be aware of the impact of each step in the journey for the customer experience (see chapter 4).

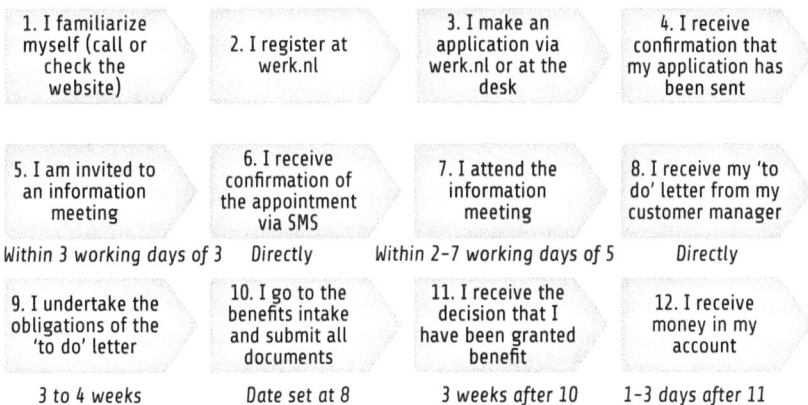

1. I familiarize myself (call or check the website)	2. I register at werk.nl	3. I make an application via werk.nl or at the desk	4. I receive confirmation that my application has been sent
5. I am invited to an information meeting	6. I receive confirmation of the appointment via SMS	7. I attend the information meeting	8. I receive my 'to do' letter from my customer manager
Within 3 working days of 3	*Directly*	*Within 2-7 working days of 5*	*Directly*
9. I undertake the obligations of the 'to do' letter	10. I go to the benefits intake and submit all documents	11. I receive the decision that I have been granted benefit	12. I receive money in my account
3 to 4 weeks	*Date set at 8*	*3 weeks after 10*	*1-3 days after 11*

Figure 3.5 *Detailed customer journey for benefits payment application from social services*

Detailed journey for applications for supplementary benefit
When applying for supplementary benefit from any social services department in the Netherlands (see figure 3.5), you must first register as a job seeker with the UWV organization. You do so via werk.nl. Even though the UWV is a totally different organization to the social services: if you wish to improve customer experience of the process of applying for benefit payments, the steps must also be included from the customer's perspective. After all, as soon as something goes seriously wrong in the job seeker step, you will be affected, as owner of the ben-

efit payments application process, despite you not being responsible for werk.nl. It will influence customers' assessment of this process and therefore their satisfaction after applying for benefit payments from 'your' social services department. In such cases, your department will need to consult with U W V on how to improve matters.

Detailed journey for a cataract operation

It is also interesting for hospitals to be able to see the total steps taken by a customer. When establishing the detailed journey for a cataract operation for example (see figure 3.6), there are so many steps that this too is an interesting signal. Many of the steps may well be dealt with on the same day or during a single appointment. It is however relevant to visualize them individually, as any of the steps may entail a crucial aspect for the customer experience.

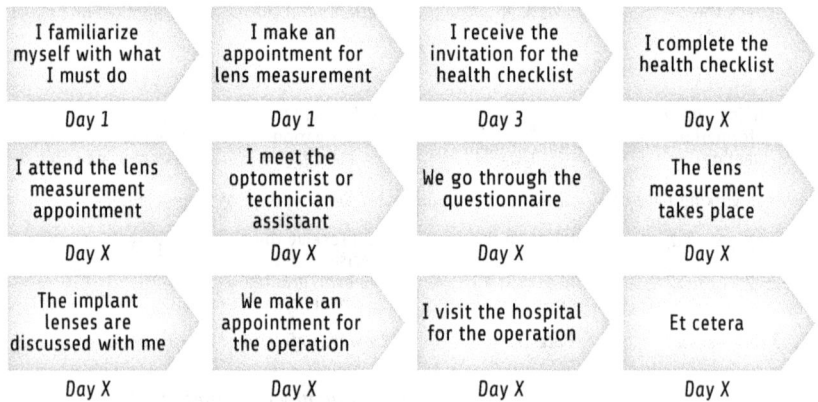

I familiarize myself with what I must do	I make an appointment for lens measurement	I receive the invitation for the health checklist	I complete the health checklist
Day 1	Day 1	Day 3	Day X
I attend the lens measurement appointment	I meet the optometrist or technician assistant	We go through the questionnaire	The lens measurement takes place
Day X	Day X	Day X	Day X
The implant lenses are discussed with me	We make an appointment for the operation	I visit the hospital for the operation	Et cetera
Day X	Day X	Day X	Day X

Figure 3.6 *Detailed customer journey of a cataract operation*

The devil is in the details

In a healthcare situation, a detailed journey was established for the process of breast cancer follow-up. This detailed journey did not identify the key issues of what went wrong from the customer's perspective. The next step was to establish the detailed journey of the dialog between the patient and doctor. Even then, the crux remained unidentified. Only when a detailed journey was established for the first ten minutes of the appointment, did the misunderstanding between the doctor's perception and that of the patient come to light. The doctor began immediately conveying information while the patient needed time to adjust, because of the tense nature of the situation. The two parties therefore failed to connect, resulting in the patient feeling uneasy and subsequently missing crucial elements of the dialog.

3.3 Customer journey as a framework for customer signals management

What we see in practice is that organizations still drown in the sea of signals, despite the structured process of customer signals management described in chapter 2. They lack a framework for effective focusing and steering of energy to those aspects which require most attention. And that is where the main customer journey fits in, as a central framework for customer signals management (see figure 3.7).

Figure 3.7 *The framework of customer signals management*

Customer contacts

You need to identify the number of customer contacts, and their context, for each step in the journey. This allows very specific improvement of that step in the journey, from both the customer and organization perspectives (see also chapter 5 on reducing costs by avoiding unnecessary customer contact moments).

Customer satisfaction

A customer satisfaction survey will be designed for each step in the customer journey (see chapter 4). By correctly designing this survey based on the detailed journey, you can determine exactly which 'knobs' need to be turned in this step of the journey.

Determining the right impact

You then combine the two, to identify the precise potential for improvement in each step, in realizing happier customers while reducing costs.

TIPS & TOOLS

There is no standard customer journey

In the maelstrom of customer experience, the customer journey has also become an increasingly popular tool with which to look at services from the customer's perspective. How does a customer click through the website? What emotions are felt during the journey? What are the most important steps in the journey? These are all questions which require individual applications of the customer journey concept if they are to be answered correctly.

We often refer to *the* customer journey. But does it really exist? There are so many different types of customer journey techniques nowadays that you run the risk of them becoming a veritable tower of Babel.

Application of the customer journey
Before listing all the different variants, you may first need to determine your objective. The different variants of the customer journey offer many applications: reinforcing brand perception, channels gearing and/or reducing contacts, determining customer satisfaction drivers, innovating services, boosting efficiency.

This also applies to the softer side of customer centricity, i.e. increased internal awareness: what does it mean to truly regard your services from the customer's perspective? The role played by a customer journey process on this softer side is by no means inferior to the harder results. But which variant is required by which objective?

Variant 1: emotional journey
In the emotional journey, you conduct qualitative research among a small group of customers to identify the emotions felt by the customer during the journey. When requesting a product for example: can we locate the negative and the positive emotions? And can we turn the negative ones around and/or add extra positive ones?

Variant 2: Lean customer value stream
In a Lean-based value stream diagram, the entire process is mapped out with various actors. The customer is one of the actors, but also other departments or a system. At the risk of offending Lean experts, I must say: in my experience with Lean value stream diagrams in practice, in which the customer certainly plays a role, I have found them to be too internally focused. They are much more an internal process diagram than a customer journey. In an actual practical example, we identified twelve steps which affected customers in the customer journey, while the Lean process only contained four steps in which the customer was affected. The remaining steps concerned the internal organization and systems.

Variant 3: online journey
The online channel is becoming increasingly important, so you need to know for sure that your customers are optimally served there. During an online journey, you follow a customer's movement through your website (based on search terms, clicks, conversion and other such data). The application which I generally discover here, is that of sales funnels. Service funnels are given much less attention however, even though the same technique will render them equally profitable.

If, for example, you know that customers searching for 'change details' tend to give up in the third screen and call you instead, you can take action. This will avoid a contact moment which is irritating for the customer, expensive for the organization and also unnecessary. This is often a win-win situation between customer experience and efficiency.

Variant 4: main customer journey

Many organizations are at real risk of drowning in the sea of customer journeys. A useful starting point is the main customer journey: what steps does a customer take with your organization, at the highest level? In an insurance company for example: I become a customer, I pay a premium, I claim damages, et cetera. There are two applications within this highest level: providing an overview of the detailed journeys, and offering insight in terms of which steps are most important, gained through research and data analysis. You can then prioritize. This highest level is scarcely suitable for any other applications, as it will always be generic.

Variant 5: detailed journey per process

The detailed customer journey per process looks only at those steps taken by the customer with your organization, in that single customer process from the main journey: 'I become a customer' for example. It does so in detail. The delivery confirmation is therefore also a step in this journey. You are not determining whether a step is positive or negative, but are actually defining the existing steps.

In other words

It is not about which journey is right or wrong. Instead, the question is: what is your objective and which journey technique is most appropriate? There is no standard customer journey, but experience has shown that the correct use of a customer journey process is one of the most successful tools on the road to a (more) customer-centric organization. Very practical, simple to apply and with great impact.

The following chapter explains how to design your customer satisfaction survey on the basis of the detailed customer journey, to discover exactly in which elements of your customer journey you should invest to achieve the best possible effect.

4. STEERING CUSTOMER EXPERIENCE

If we knew what we were doing, it wouldn't be called research, would it?

— ALBERT EINSTEIN

Too many customer satisfaction surveys are conducted which fail to answer the question: which knobs must I turn to improve customer experience? Yet any organization can design its survey in order to immediately be able to start improving aspects which have actual impact on the customers' experience.

4.1 CSAT, NPS, CES ... which will it be?

Customer Satisfaction (CSAT), the Net Promoter Score (NPS) and the Customer Effort Score (CES) are all commonly used as indicators for customer experience. So let's go back to square one: why are we measuring that? Because organizations want loyal customers. For commercial organizations, loyal customers mean more turnover: more sales per customer, more enduring customer relationships and mouth-to-mouth advertising for new customers. For public sector organizations, loyalty means trust: a relationship between the general public and the government in which a dialog is possible. This prevents continuous escalation to parties such as an ombudsman, due to the relationship being marked only by mistrust. The million-dollar question remains: which knob is the most important to turn if I am to increase this loyalty and trust?

Customer satisfaction

One of the most persistent convictions since the arrival of the NPS is that customer satisfaction does not matter, that satisfied customers still move on. However, it is the degree of satisfaction that counts. Customers who score you a 7 are satisfied, but could indeed easily switch to some other organization. However, customers scoring an 8 or higher, have a strong relationship and loyal behavior. This has been proven in many studies over the years (incl. Van der Aa, 2011) looking at the relationship between satisfaction and loyalty, and that relationship is still ongoing. The measurement of satisfaction is a perfect instrument with which to improve customer experience, but you need to ensure your customers score you 8 or higher, when looking to create loyal customers or increase trust.

Net Promoter Score

The Net Promoter Score (Reichheld, 2006) is a percentage calculated on the basis of the score for the question: "How likely are you to recommend company X to friends or family?" on a scale of 0 to 10. The percentage of customers scoring 0 through 6 (the detractors) is deducted from the percentage of customers scoring 9 or 10 (the promoters). Due to the largest group (7 and 8) not being included, the NPS is seen to fluctuate greatly in practice. The NPS may be -10 in the first quarter and +20 in the second quarter, without reasons becoming known. This makes it very difficult to steer customer experience. Another disadvantage of the NPS is that it does not use model analyses, but rather reasons which are requested from the customers themselves. If you ask customers what is important, you run the risk of focusing on the wrong aspects (see box 'Latent needs').

Customer Effort Score

A new indicator came into being in 2013, the Customer Effort Score (Dixon, 2013): "How much effort did you have to make to ...?" The dot dot dot concerns a certain transaction: buy a product, get my question answered, and so on. The authors indicate that customers are not at all interested in receiving a bunch of flowers and having their expectations exceeded, but that the crux of good customer experience lies in the sense of convenience. They have conducted extensive research into the customer experience in contact center environments, of that you must be aware. While the sense of convenience is absolutely important, the question is whether this is also the case outside the context of customer service. In the satisfaction surveys sketched below, you can certainly include convenience and measure its impact. Convenience really matters after all, though the degree depends entirely on the branch, organization, process, channel and target group.

	Pros	Cons
CSAT	· Each respondent knows the score · Applicable in every branch · Strong relation with loyalty · Central scientific role	· Not 'sexy' enough, score remains unchanged too long · Incorrect image: weak relation with loyalty · Focus on latent needs
NPS (eNPS, gNPS)	· Puts customer experience on the map · Strong relation with loyalty	· Fluctuates greatly due to percentage calculation · Not applicable in all branches · No focus on latent needs
CES (2.0)	· Practical application by examining everything through the spectacles of convenience · Can be greatly improved, through communication alone.	· Only possible per transaction · Is a driver of NPS/CSAT · Difficult formulation

Table 4.1 *Pros and cons of* CSAT, NPS *and* CES

Science

The pros and cons of the various metrics determine when you should apply which one (see table 4.1). But what does science say about the relationship between these three metrics? It says that loyalty is always preceded by customer satisfaction (Van der Aa, 2011). Commitment and trust also play a role in the relationship between satisfaction and loyalty. They are both boosted when satisfaction is increased, and in turn they boost loyalty. Satisfaction therefore has both a direct and indirect positive impact on loyalty. Word-of-mouth advertising (which essentially is the NPS question) is only one of the two components of the scientific definition of true loyalty. True loyalty also includes the intention to make a repeat purchase from the organization. NPS is not equal to loyalty therefore. You cannot create loyal customers without this being preceded by a sense of satisfaction. Due to the Customer Effort Score preceding loyalty, and satisfaction nestling in between the two, this also means that the Customer Effort Score is a driver for satisfaction. The convenience of the service determines my satisfaction with the service. The easier it is, the higher my score and therefore the steadier my loyalty. And so the three metrics are strongly interrelated. Due to the central role played by customer satisfaction, customer signals management uses this network to steer customer experience.

Common sense

Day-to-day business is what counts in the end, along with measurably improved customer services. The essence is important therefore, namely that you have a system which works as follows: you measure a score, you analyze the causes, you improve the causes and you measure a higher score. If the mechanism works – whether it be CSAT, NPS or CES – please stick to the method you are using, as we know all three to be interrelated. If, on the other hand, you discover that your choice of interventions does not boost your score (any longer), there is a good chance that your method is failing you somewhere. The tips given in this chapter may then help you to identify effective interventions with measurable results.

Latent needs make or break customer perception

While studies concerning the role of our subconscious do not entirely concur, they all quote an influencing factor between 75 percent and 95 percent. Given the magnitude of that role, why do the vast majority of surveys aimed at improving customer experience explicitly ask customers what matters to them? This article is a wholehearted argument in favor of a different approach. One which has been proven to work in practice.

Science, research, statistics. They're tricky, abstract terms for many people. I never refer to myself as a scientist or researcher, but rather a pragmatic improver. The pragmatism lies in a constant linking of matters which quite simply work in practice. Having learned just enough of the scientific world during my Ph.D. and just enough of the system of organizational management in my day-to-day experience, I am able to combine the two and improve customer experience. The guiding principle is to tangibly measure your customers' latent needs.

Don't ask about customer importance

Virtually all NPS or customer satisfaction methodologies ask customers about the root cause of any particular score. Such surveys also enquire about the importance attached to a certain step in the journey or to a touchpoint. In doing so, they increase the risk of you concentrating on the wrong improvement points. And (help) explain why many companies fail to boost satisfaction or their NPS.

For example: On asking customers what can be improved in a contact center setting, their answers will often make some reference to the awful selection menus (conscious reaction). So if that's where you want to improve satisfaction, this methodology will have you tackling this process.

If, on the other hand, you can identify your customers' latent needs (unconscious reaction), the selection menu will prove to be largely insignificant. The human domain then suddenly takes precedence, in the employee who listens effectively, showing empathy for their situation and immediately giving the right answer (first time fix). In this case therefore, you would have wrongly invested your valuable energy; namely in the selection menu.

Instead, ask for their appreciation

Another example concerns the importance of the feeling gained from an organization (personal attention, empathy, et cetera). When consciously questioned, this came fourth on the list. When subconsciously questioned, it had the greatest impact on satisfaction by far. Forget about asking customers about importance therefore, and ask about their appreciation. Then apply statistics (no, not correlations, but rather cause and effect analyses!) to objectively determine which latent needs define their satisfaction.

You will then know exactly which knobs to turn, and will see a customer process score improve from 7.1 to 7.5 within a three-month pilot, thanks to two really simple yet extremely direct and effective adjustments which anyone can implement, at no cost. Imagine if you were to adjust even more elements in a number of processes which really matter to your customers. In another organization, this resulted in a score growth from 6.8 to 8 in three months' time.

Emotion or transaction?
So is it only emotion which counts? Absolutely not! Latent needs are just as likely to be transactional. And so you can arrive at that 8 or higher customer satisfaction score needed to actually create loyal customers, through both emotion and transaction. Today's digital possibilities will serve to make transactions even smarter, quicker and more personal. The crux is to use statistics to become conscious of the customer's subconscious experience and needs.

Let's get to work!
Statistics, science, doesn't that all take years? Not at all, you can identify these latent needs for your customer process or channel within four weeks. You simply need to adhere strictly to the detailed journey from a customer perspective when compiling your questionnaire. By including both transaction and emotion, you can rest assured that you are in control and that measurable results are just around the corner. Enjoy!

4.2   Prioritization from the customer's perspective

The million-dollar question in all this is what to steer for customer experience, how to choose the right knobs. It is a dual phase process: you begin by determining which steps of the main journey play the greatest role for customers, and then move on to discover which knobs affect satisfaction in each step of the journey.

Determining which steps matter most
Most main customer journeys (see figure 4.1) comprise approximately ten steps. Not all organizations are ready to start with the end-to-end journey at once, but want to start with a few processes that matter the most. If that's the case in your organization, you need to know which of these steps should have priority, from the customer's point of view. Using a three-point plan, you can design a survey to answer precisely that question.

Step 1. Formulation of the questionnaire and conducting the survey;
Step 2. Analysis of the results;
Step 3. Validation with supplementary data.

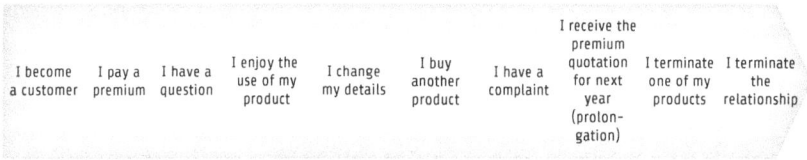

I become a customer	I pay a premium	I have a question	I enjoy the use of my product	I change my details	I buy another product	I have a complaint	I receive the premium quotation for next year (prolon-gation)	I terminate one of my products	I terminate the relationship

Figure 4.1 *Example of main customer journey*

Step 1 – Formulation of the questionnaire and conducting the survey
Start by conducting a survey among a general random sample of cus-tomers, to whom you ask three questions:
1. How satisfied are you with organization X?
2. Which of the following elements of organization X's services con-tributed most to your score? (Choose maximum 3 reasons).
   a. Here, you summarize the ten steps of the customer journey.
3. Which ones stood out for you [name of the step]? (Choose maxi-mum 3 reasons).
   a. Here, you summarize five to ten specific items per step.
   For the 'becoming a customer' step for example, this can include items such as:
   – simplicity of the registration form
   – speed of receiving the offer
   – accuracy of the offer
   – friendliness of the employee
   – suitability for my requirements
   – et cetera

This questionnaire is then conducted among a large random selec-tion of customers, so that you receive at least two hundred com-pleted questionnaires per target group. If you have commercial and private customers who receive different services, they are two target groups – therefore also with two customer journeys and two ques-tionnaires. In this survey, you will not be selecting customers with whom a transaction has recently taken place, but rather a general random sample of all active customers. Considering the average response of 15 to 20 percent, you will need to approach at least 1500 customers.

Step 2 – analysis of the results
When processing the results, you only count the number of times that a customer process is named. In this phase, it is unimportant whether the satisfaction score is positive or negative. You simply look at the number of times that customers have named the steps, as an explanation for the score. The overall tendency in this phase is to focus on the customer processes which result in the most negative scores. And nearly everyone will tend to try to improve the lowest score in a satisfaction survey. Yet it may well have much greater effect on total satisfaction if you can improve the 7 for friendliness, making it a 9. You always need to watch out for blind spots, when concentrating only on negative scores. In this phase, you can assume that the customer processes named most often, are those most relevant to the total experience of your organization.

Step 3 – Validation with supplementary data
One risk of this approach is that you rely fully on the customer's judgment and may therefore end up with a wrong top 3. (Remember the selection menu which had no objective impact on satisfaction but was named by everyone?) You therefore need to validate the top 3 from this survey using other data. This is done by checking how many customers take the various steps annually. How many of them become customers? How many customers have submitted a complaint? How many customers call us? And so on. This is based on the idea that the greater the number of customers who follow a certain process annually, the greater the role of that process in the total customer experience of your organization. By overlaying the two results, you have a good foundation for solid prioritization from the customer's perspective.

4.3 Choosing the knobs per step in the customer journey

Thanks to the previous step, you have now identified the most relevant customer processes in the journey and can start designing the surveys required to choose the knobs for each step in the main journey. The method used to design the surveys is always the same, and comprises four steps:
1. Formulating the questionnaire
2. Conducting the survey
3. Choosing the knobs
4. Reporting the top 10 items

Step 1 – Formulating the questionnaire

To begin with, you establish the detailed customer journey as described in chapter 3. Together with all the people who play a role in this journey, you take a detailed look at the steps taken by the customer. Now describe the existing customer process and keep probing what the customer actually experiences, to make sure you are not including internal process steps. The questionnaire can be formulated on the basis of these steps. For each step in the detailed journey, put yourself in the customer's shoes and formulate statements on the services concerned with that step. A statement on the delivery confirmation, for example, could be 'the delivery confirmation was clear'. And in the step in which a customer visits the office, a statement could be 'the employee at the desk was friendly'. Don't limit yourself to a single question per step, instead ask all questions which you believe to play a role in the customer's experience. These can be both functional (turnaround time, waiting time, etc.) and emotional items (friendliness, respect, etc.; See also paragraph 6.5). Now send these draft questionnaires back to everyone involved in the journey for review, and you're ready to conduct the survey.

Dutch people do not score a 9 or 10
The Net Promoter Score is the subject of great discussion on why it is possibly not applicable. One of the reasons is apparently culturally determined. The

9 and 10 scores are relevant when working with the NPS, as they are essential in calculating the percentage. Organizations in the Netherlands who do not score well according to the NPS often blame this on the 'average Dutch person' never scoring a 9 or 10. Within the context of debunking myths (see chapter 6), this too has been tested in practice. During satisfaction surveys for customer service telephony, no less than 30 percent of the customers scored organizations a 10! And so we can add yet another reason to the list: apparently you have yet to do the right things to make a difference for your customers...

Step 2 – Conducting the survey

Once the questionnaire is complete, the time is ripe to distribute it among your customers. The closer you are to the moment of the transaction, the better the results. When monitoring the process of becoming a customer, you do so among recently registered customers. When monitoring the process of customer service telephony, you do so among customers who have recently called.

What is recent?

Recent is not a set period of time, but it should never be longer than a month ago. A week is often good timing, also in terms of response. Directly after the contact or transaction is not always the preferable option. You need to be aware of what you are measuring. Telephone contact is probably the best example. If you conduct the survey directly after the contact (via a computer, for example), you will only measure the conversation the customer just had. This can be very valuable in providing your employees with feedback on how customers assess them. If you conduct the survey a week later, it will measure the total customer service experience. An employee will often promise to undertake a certain action during the call. When monitoring directly after the call, the customer has no idea whether that promise will be kept. A week after the contact, most actions will have been taken and customers can therefore effectively assess the total service process. In virtually all cases, the score directly after the contact is considerably higher than a week after the contact. This is due to the employees almost always scoring well (also a week later) and the assumption being made directly after the contact, that their promise will be kept.

Conditions for conducting the survey

There are all kinds of tools at your disposal nowadays to simply conduct such questionnaires among your customers, using e-mail, qr codes, info pedestals, WhatsApp, etc. Due to this initial questionnaire being quite lengthy, e-mail is nearly always the first choice. It's therefore essential to have as many e-mail addresses of your customers as possible. Also important is that you can make the right selection of customers who have recently undertaken customer process X or followed channel Y. Take a close look at the available data and selection options before starting the survey. When planning to conduct more than one survey, also give careful thought to the exclusion of customers from surveys. That too is easily facilitated by most tools nowadays. You do not want customers to receive multiple questionnaires within a brief period of time. Customers are often excluded from further surveys for three to six months.

Step 3 – Choosing the knobs

You will have received a response within a week or two, and can now apply the data in so-called driver analyses. This is the phase in which you discover which knobs to turn to improve your customers' experience.

Forget correlation analyses

The reports provided by most research agencies include a so-called priorities matrix. Figure 4.2 shows an example. Research agencies base this matrix on correlations, and many items can be seen to be grouped in the center. This is because correlations do not allow actual cause and consequence analyses to be made. Take care therefore to make the correct analyses or have them made. The process begins with a factor analysis, followed by regression analysis using the identified factors.

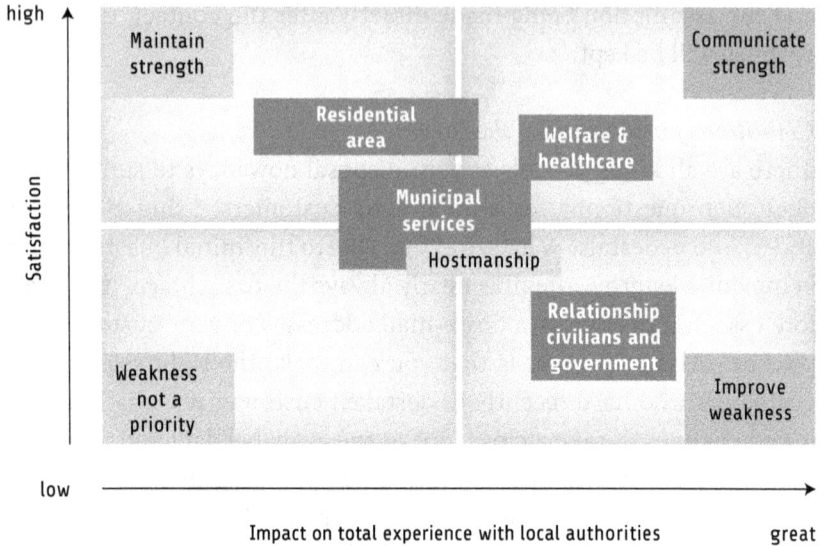

Figure 4.2 *Fictional example of correlation analysis*

Interpreting the driver analysis

Statistical data is a pretty complex subject matter for many people. A number of elements are relevant in recognizing how statistics can help you steer for customer experience in practice. They are not difficult to fathom once you see the practical relevance. You do not need to know how statistics works, but rather understand the significance of the statistic results. In other words, how to interpret them. An example (see figure 4.3) shows which relevant steering information can be extrapolated from a driver analysis.

Insight 1: grouping from the customer's perspective. The first step in which statistical data helps you, is in grouping the statements from the questionnaire. Let's imagine that your questionnaire has 25 statements, the factor analysis ensures that they are grouped as your customers believe they should be. This grouping may therefore be totally at odds with the questionnaire, which you have grouped on the basis of the customer journey steps. Your questionnaire grouping is therefore actually quite irrelevant, as the factor analysis will show how statements should be grouped together from the customer's perspec-

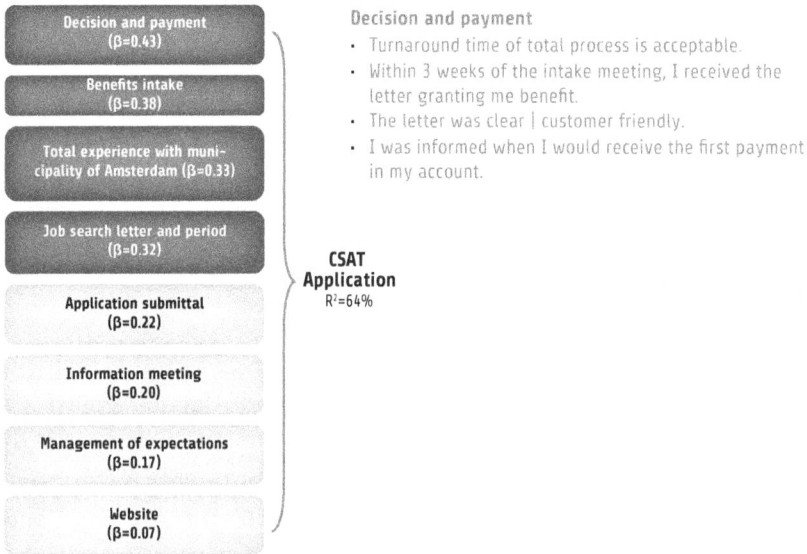

Decision and payment
(β=0.43)

Benefits intake
(β=0.38)

Total experience with muni-
cipality of Amsterdam (β=0.33)

Job search letter and period
(β=0.32)

Application submittal
(β=0.22)

Information meeting
(β=0.20)

Management of expectations
(β=0.17)

Website
(β=0.07)

Decision and payment
- Turnaround time of total process is acceptable.
- Within 3 weeks of the intake meeting, I received the letter granting me benefit.
- The letter was clear | customer friendly.
- I was informed when I would receive the first payment in my account.

CSAT
Application
R^2=64%

Figure 4.3 *Example of driver analysis*

tive – thus showing latent needs. It's fascinating to see which aspects really matter.

Insight 2: asking the right questions. One of the great weaknesses of many surveys is that the questionnaires are a hodgepodge of questions which various people want to ask the customer. In healthcare for example, it is a compromise between healthcare insurers, healthcare providers and patient associations. Even within organizations themselves, you can sometimes recognize a negotiation between various departments. They have no notion of whether the questions posed are actually questions which the customer believes important. The driver analysis tells you this. In figure 4.3, R^2 = 64%, in which R^2 stands for explained variance, which in turn defines the reliability of your model. In this case, it says that you can influence 64 percent of the satisfaction with the application process using these eight factors. 64 percent is extremely high. Scientifically speaking, 20 or 30 percent is sometimes already high, but in practice you apply a bottom limit of 40 percent. If the explained variance drops below 40 percent, you have omitted certain aspects which customers believe to be truly important. Experience has shown questionnaires formulated on the basis of the detailed customer journey to result in extremely reliable models, often with unexplained variants of 50 to 70. This means that you can skip the qualitative sessions with customers, as long as you can establish a good detailed customer journey. It is not until the explained variance drops below 40 percent, that you need to return to the drawing board and it becomes useful to involve your customers in order to identify what you have missed.

Insight 3: impact of the knobs. The most important aspect is that you know which knobs to turn in order to improve satisfaction. Figure 4.3 shows that there are eight factors ('knobs') which you can turn. 'Appraisal and payment' scores (β =0.43) and 'Website' scores (β =0.07). This means that improving the statements given for 'Appraisal and payment' will have no less than six times the effect of improving the statements given for 'Website'. In other words, if you have 10,000 dollars available for improving customer satisfaction, it is six times better spent on improving the appraisal and benefits payment process rather than improving the website. And so you know the exact importance of the various themes and where you can best focus your energy.

Insight 4: what doesn't matter. This factor analysis also shows that certain items don't matter. It allows you to objectively assess customer reactions to all kinds of myths, also directly ridding you of all the internal discussions on what is really important to customers. A great example of this occurred at a social services department. There was a conviction, internally, that submitting documentary proof when requesting supplementary benefit was a very tedious activity for customers. They were so certain of this that policy documents had already been prepared, requiring less/no documentary proof to be provided. The situation was then assessed in the model analysis, and what did it show? This aspect not only had low impact, but was actually even insignificant for customers. Once again, we see how crucial it is to constantly check with our customers, simply because we are all customers and we each have our own colored images of what we like and dislike.

Insight 5: check target group differences. As long as you can fine tune the model analysis knobs, and the level of satisfaction continues to increase, there is no reason to further differentiate into target groups. It will only be useful to look more closely at target groups if you observe the satisfaction growth curve to be stagnating, while you are certain that all improvements have been implemented effectively.

It is however useful to distinguish between target groups who give differing results for crucial processes; an insurance company may distinguish between customers whose claim has been accepted and those which have not. Or a social services department whose customers' applications for benefit have been granted or rejected. Using virtually the same questionnaire – the process is often comparable after all – you simply need to redo the model analysis using data from the other customer group. In the social services example, the 'total experience with local authorities' factor was by far the number 1 impact on the satisfaction of rejected customers, while this factor was at number 3 among customers whose application had been approved. This factor includes more emotional aspects, such as the sense of promises being kept, availability for customer questions and respectful treatment. These obviously become considerably more important for rejected customers.

The KANO model versus model analyses

Noriaki Kano (Kano, 1984) developed the so-called KANO model for customer satisfaction (see figure 4.4). His model distinguishes between three types of drivers for customer satisfaction:

- *Satisfiers*: if the organization does not implement these (effectively), they have hardly any negative impact on customer satisfaction, but if they are fully implemented by the organization, they have a strong positive impact on customer satisfaction.
- *Dissatisfiers*: if the organization does not implement these (effectively), they have a strong negative impact on customer satisfaction, but if they are fully implemented by the organization, they have hardly any positive impact on customer satisfaction.
- *Performance indicators*: if the organization does not implement these (effectively), they have a negative impact on customer satisfaction, but

if they are fully implemented by the organization, they have a positive impact on customer satisfaction.

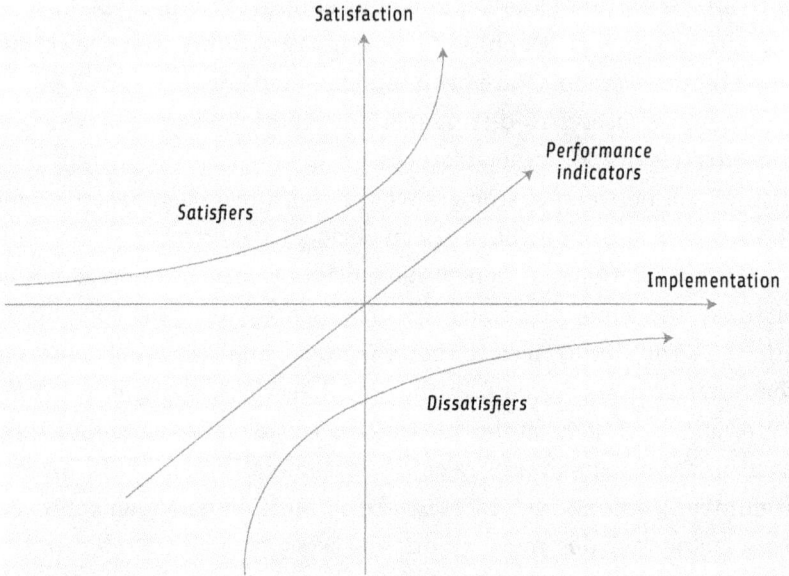

Figure 4.4 KANO model

More and more organizations use these satisfier and dissatisfier terms, but without having investigated which items are satisfiers or not. In order to investigate this, apply the following statements to each item which you believe to play a role (Matzler, Fuchs and Schubert, 2004):

1. The functional form: how do you feel about having direct telephone contact with an employee?
2. The dysfunctional form: how do you feel about not having direct telephone contact with an employee?

The reply categories for each one are: 'I really want that', 'I expect that', 'it makes no difference to me', 'I find it distracting'. By comparing the two forms, you then know under which of the three types of indicators the item should be classified.

In the example of the selection menu, you know by now that it can be risky to ask customers to judge the importance of certain items. What's more, this method does not show you the exact impact of the items, you have no insight into the latent factors and whether you are asking all the right questions from the customer's perspective, unlike the model analyses which do provide that information. Model analyses should therefore have preference over the KANO approach.

Step 4 – Reporting the top 10 items

Although the descriptions of the factors may still be vague ('appraisal and payment'), they will take shape in this step. Using another statistical analysis, you can further specify the factors to find the exact items within the most important factors that make the difference. These items are so specific that it is very easy to develop relevant improvements to increase the appraisal on these items. Finally, you combine the score of the items with the impact of the items and you know exactly how to make a high impact difference with low impact investment.

The items are so well specified at this level that they can be implemented immediately. This is also the point at which you can combine any qualitative research with the quantitative survey already conducted, in the model analysis. If, for example, the organization has no idea of how to make the letter clearer or friendlier, customers could be asked their opinion. Though employees generally know full well what needs to be improved. It is often an internal battle between various departments, such as Marketing, Legal affairs and IT, which results in letters lacking clarity and friendliness.

Channels versus customer processes

The complete process of identifying the knobs to turn, as sketched here for the customer processes, applies to the channels in exactly the same way. There too, you need to design questionnaires and driver analyses. You generate a separate questionnaire for each channel, allowing you to identify the most important knobs per channel. For validated questionnaires with the drivers of e-mail and thelephone, see http://ksmfactory.com/en/blog-en/win-win-win-the-10-questions-for-e-mail-and-telephony/

4.4   Sense and nonsense of continuous monitoring

The trend in monitoring satisfaction is increasingly shifting towards continuous monitoring. Is that always sensible? When and when not?

Frequency of driver analyses

A driver analyses does not require frequent reassessment. The impact of the factors only changes once you have made serious improvement efforts, and the speed of improvement is not exactly high within most organizations, making reassessment every two to three years more than sufficient. But always wait to do so until you are certain that substantial improvements have been implemented, which will increase customer satisfaction by a full report point. Only then can you see the knobs changing. The model analysis was carried out at an organization, and showed the waiting time on the telephone to be one of the most important knobs. There were indeed serious problems with waiting times at that point, which were running up to 30 minutes and more. Once these waiting times had been shortened, not only did the satisfaction score increase by a full report point, but the impact of the waiting times was considerably lower. Now that the waiting times had been sorted, other matters important to the customer became apparent, which is in line with many studies showing that waiting time is net the most important driver. Thus the impact of the factors can shift over time, depending on the adjustments made in your services.

Frequency of satisfaction monitoring

There's a big difference between continuous monitoring and continuous analysis. The advantage of continuous monitoring is that you are constantly on top of the moment of customer experience, which will give much more reliable results. Moreover, you can check whether the interventions have had an effect, without having to wait 12 months for a new survey and the chance to steer your processes. Continuous monitoring is certainly preferable therefore. But don't be tempted to continuously analyze. The tools available today give us all real-time insight into the figures, and there is a risk that the entire organization is driven crazy by the scores. If you truly want to take action on points which matter, make sure you have effective reporting of the scores, insights and main priorities on a quarterly basis. After all, a three-month improvement cycle is very speedy in organizations not accustomed to making end-to-end improvements. The analysis frequency also depends entirely on the response. When monitoring a minor customer process and receiving 10 completed questionnaires per month (30 is the minimum for statistically relevant conclusions), there is little sense in quarterly analysis. Every six months or yearly will suffice.

Size does matter

The length of questionnaires is a popular subject for discussion, especially since the arrival of online reviewing systems which often rely on a single question and a single open response. Remember, this phase is all about identifying the knobs which you can turn. This means that you should preferably be using too many statements rather than too few. (Twenty to thirty statements are often required for processes, and ten to twenty for channels). You can always scrap a number after generating the model, once you know what matters and what not. All kinds of tests have also been conducted to measure response, which is generally between 10 and 30 percent for this style of questionnaire. There is no difference in the response rate between shorter and longer questionnaires. There is however a difference in the response rate between customer processes with a greater or lesser impact on customers. At an insurance company, the response rate for questionnaires concerning claims was 30, while it was only 8 for the process of becoming a customer. After all, submitting a damages claim has much more impact on a customer than requesting car insurance. It is also a myth that only customers with a strongly negative experience respond. The score for the claims questionnaire was more than 8. When considering the enormous value of knowing exactly what to do to improve customer experience and of generating great response, the length of the questionnaire should never be a point of discussion. Only after having found the max top 10 items that drive satisfaction, you can reduce the questionnaire to consist of these items in the continuous measurements.

Balancing act

The driver analysis provides you with information on which elements play the greatest role for improvement, and even gives the top improvement points. Once the model analysis is complete, you therefore don't need to keep using the complete questionnaire, but can simply apply a shorter version containing the points for improvement and the satisfaction question. Think carefully about whether you require trending information for other questions. Use this to formulate a shorter version of the questionnaire which can be continuously put to customers.

Doesn't that all sound logical?

Now you might be thinking: "Do we really need such detailed monitoring, even though we all really know what's important to customers? We're all human after all." Yes and no. There are two reasons why this type of driver analysis monitoring is so vital. Firstly, because you sometimes really make the wrong assumptions of what customers believe important (remember the provision of documents when applying for supplementary benefit?). Secondly, because there are so many issues in your context, which you must justify in order to improve customer experience results. This method of monitoring brings everyone properly to the helm of customer experience and allows you to get the entire organization on board for the reasons behind the essential improvement. In an organization accustomed to steering for cold hard results, it is an essential component for mobilization in the direction of a theme often shrouded in the mists of vagueness.

Customer satisfaction using driver analyses is one axis of steering customer experience, the reduction of costs is the other axis. The following chapter describes how customer signals management translates customer experience into dollars.

5

REDUCING COSTS THROUGH CUSTOMER EXPERIENCE

Wise men don't need advice. Fools won't take it.

— BENJAMIN FRANKLIN

Being able to steer satisfaction in order to improve customer experience is one of the key issues of customer signals management. The other is how an improved customer experience can also reduce costs. The surefire location for a win-win situation between improved customer experience and reduced costs is found in the customer contact center. After all, customers don't want to make three calls if one will suffice, or if they can do something themselves. On the other hand, the organization can avoid two or three contact moments and therefore save costs. A win-win situation for both parties.

5.1 Customer experience and unnecessary customer contact

Studies (Dixon, 2013; Van der Aa, 2011) have shown customer contact to play an important role in customer loyalty. Satisfaction about the contact is strongly related to satisfaction about the organization as a whole, to commitment to the organization, trust in the organization and loyalty towards the organization. This all concerns the moment at which the customer seeks contact with the organization. At that point, you must be there for the customer and handle that specific contact moment very well.

However, satisfaction about the contact is not the same as whether or not that contact is desirable. If I am a customer calling because my invoice is unclear, or I have not been called back as promised, that contact moment will affect my satisfaction. While the contact moment itself may go well, I would of course have preferred an unambiguous invoice or a telephone call from an employee if that was promised (see also 'Win-win-win' box).

Win-win-win

A recent survey conducted for an insurance company showed that customers who themselves found the contact to be avoidable, were significantly less satisfied about the telephone contact than customers who believed the contact moment to be unavoidable. The same applied to customers whose question was not handled in one go. There is therefore a threefold gain to be had in more efficient services in the customer journey: happier customers because of more first time fixes, even happier customers who do not need to make the call, and cost reduction for each telephone call thus avoided. For e-mail contact too, customers who believed contact to be avoidable were significantly less satisfied than customers who indicated that the contact moment was unavoidable.

Moreover, an increasing number of studies show that customers wish to arrange matters themselves. If they meet obstacles, they want there to be an opportunity for contact. There are great gains to be had therefore, both in customer experience and in (reduced) costs for the organization. This can be done by focusing on the existing customer contact moments, in order to determine which contact moments are undesirable for both customers and the organization, and can be avoided. The cause of such undesirable customer contact often lies in the end-to-end customer journey where something goes wrong. And so the customer-centric approach is once again key to avoiding customer contact.

5.2   Customer signals management business case

The perspective of customer contact moments offers the opportunity to quickly and simply generate a business case for customer signals management. You do so on the basis of the following three steps:

1. Establish the annual number of customer contact moments
Check which types of customer contact your organization has: telephone, e-mail, complaints, objections and appeals, visits to the office or store, web care, chat, and so on. Make sure you derive the total number of contact moments per year from the management information, per type of customer contact. Let's assume you then arrive at an overview that you have 1,000,000 telephone calls, 200,000 e-mails and 50,000 complaints.

2. Calculate the costs per customer contact moment
The costs vary per type of customer contact moment. A good indication of the costs per contact moment will often already be available within the organization. If not, there are a number of benchmarks, as sketched in chapter 3: a telephone call costs 10 dollars, an e-mail 15 dollars and a complaint 75 dollars. In your example, the total amount of costs per customer contact moment per year is then:

(1,000,000 × 10 dollars) + (200,000 × 15 dollars) + (50,000 × 75 dollars) = 16,750,000 dollars.

3. Estimate the percentage of unnecessary contact
In order to determine how much budget is available for customer signals management, you determine what percentage of customer contact moments could be avoided. The pragmatic approach is to assume that you can avoid 5 percent of these contact moments by improving the customer experience: these are the unnecessary customer contact moments. After all, this is a percentage which everyone believes feasible, thus keeping you clear of lengthy discussions about the percentage itself. The company will therefore be saving 837,500 dollars in costs per year. In other words: you have 837,500 dollars available for investment in improving services, and this investment will be earned

back within a year. And you often will not need anywhere near such an amount in order to implement customer signals management.

5.3 Determine the actual percentage of unnecessary contact

Making an estimation for the business case is a good way of getting a sense of the potential offered by avoidance of unnecessary contact moments. But what is the actual potential of customer-centric improvements of your services? The simplest solution when confronted with this question is to ask the customers themselves. They are the perfect starting point from which to determine where unnecessary customer contact moments can be found.

Ask the customer

Most contact centers periodically measure their customers' satisfaction with telephone and/or e-mail contact. All you have to do in this case is add two questions:

1. Was your question answered in one go? If not, what could we have done to have answered it in one go? (open question)
2. Do you believe this contact moment could have been avoided? If so, what could we have done? (open question)

The percentage of customers answering 'yes' to question 2, is a perfect indication of the potential contact moments which even the customers feel could have been avoided. That will often will often lie between 20 and 30 percent. Let alone if you further innovate your services beyond customers' baseline expectations. The open answers to this question immediately provide a direction for your quest. Take care not to add up the percentages of questions 1 and 2 together, as there will of course be an overlap. Many of the customers who report that their question was not answered in one go, will also indicate that the contact was avoidable. However, the percentage of customers who feel the contact was avoidable will always be higher than the percentage of first-time fixes. By splitting the two, you will know exactly which share is attributed to repeat traffic and which share lies in the customer journey.

Always consider both the contact and the journey.
One of the most important challenges in this type of process is the internal steering of the end-to-end journey and mobilization of those causing the contact. After all, the contact center incurs costs for dealing with contact moments, even though it is not the department causing the contact. The only contact moments caused by the contact center itself are the repeat traffic due to incorrectly answered questions. The contact center must reduce that number itself. In terms of potential for improvement, it is often no more than 10 to 15 percent. The other causers can be found along the journey. The online department, which has developed an overly complex login process, causing customers to call. The marketing department, which has marketed a product about which customers call with questions. The invoicing department, which works with incomprehensible calculations. Et cetera. All of them are departments outside the contact center. Ensure that you very quickly gain objective information on the cause of contact moments, to enable an effective dialog with each other.

5.4 Smart contact registration

Contact registration is unmissable if you are to get a good sense of the number of contact moments and their subjects. Although you know beforehand that it is impossible to correctly register 100 percent of all contact moments, not registering them is not an option when looking to improve customer experience and reduce costs.

Classification of the contact registration
The crux of contact registration lies in finding a balance between three matters:
1. the employee who understands what he must fill in, while not taking too much time to do so;
2. the organization departments who need to understand when the process concerns them;
3. understanding the actual cause of the contact moment; what is the customer's question?

Three levels of registration often work best. Level 1 often concerns the process, level 2 concerns a product and level 3 the customer's subject or question. If the contact registration system is new or can be simply adapted, it is certainly worthwhile applying the customer journey classification. Level 1 is the step in the main journey (becoming a customer), level 2 the steps within that journey (the online application form) and level 3 the subject or customer's question (confirmation not received). But even if the existing contact registration system bears no resemblance to the customer journey steps, it is still useful to plot the various registration subjects in the journey. You can then identify those steps in which the most gains are to be made.

Sense and nonsense of contact registration
On implementing contact registration, you'll soon discover many challenges in the effective design of a registration process. They are found not so much in the content of the levels, but much more in steering the registration process and making use of the registration data. If contact center employees constantly hear that their processing time has priority over the registration process, you can bet your bottom dollar that registration will not always take place (effectively). Instead, make sure the contact center is steered towards registration of at least 80 percent of the contact moments. If the employees then never hear anything about what happens with the registration data, you should not be surprised if a substantial percentage of the data concerns the first subject, as it is the quickest after all. And you can also be almost certain that the real customer question cannot be derived from the data. So why is it so important? You need cold hard results concerning the scope of the number of contact moments. You can then make the departments causing those contact moments aware of what they're doing, and gain enough priority to actually have them take action. Figures and dollars still work best. If the contact center indicates that 100,000 telephone calls are received annually as the result of ambiguous calculations on invoices, at 10 dollars per telephone call, we're talking serious amounts of money. This justifies serious one-off investment, as these are annual costs which can be avoided.

The real customer question

There are many smart and speedy possibilities nowadays when it comes to discovering the real customer question. Nearly all organizations must record conversations due to compliance and/or quality considerations. The customer question soon becomes apparent from such conversations. One of the most effective ways of working is if you can link the registration to the recordings. You can then quite simply retrieve five hundred recordings from the system for the 'product X, cancellation, cancellation status' theme. You spend two hours together with the project team, dividing the five hundred recordings among groups of two, and instructing everyone to do nothing more than type the literal customer question in an Excel sheet. After each question, they can move directly to the following recording, as it is not the quality of the conversation which counts at this point, but purely the customer question. You can therefore easily work through these five hundred conversations in a two-hour period. It will give immediate and clear insight into a) whether the registration is correct and b) the nature of the actual customer question behind the subject. Employees can be provided with feedback on the registration process and you can immediately start to discover the actual causes of the contact moments (see also chapter 7).

5.5 Avoiding unnecessary customer contact

Generally speaking, there are four opportunities for avoiding contact deemed undesirable by a customer:
1. The quality of the contact moment itself
2. End-to-end improvement of the customer journey
3. Online facilitation
4. Proactively answering questions

1. The quality of the contact moment itself
These are the contact moments which cannot be processed in one go. They require 'repeat traffic' rather than being a 'first time fix'. These are contact moments which the contact center itself can avoid, by better training of employees, for example. What you often see here is that organizations determine the percentage of repeat traffic by hav-

ing employees note whether or not the contact moment was a first time fix. The same employees are then issued a target for the percentage of first time fix contact moments. Here lies the risk of inaccurate management information, as the employee makes a subjective estimation of whether the customer's problem has been solved, and has a vested interest in collecting as many 'first time fixes' as possible. It is therefore important to (also) always ask the customer whether his problem was solved in one go. Once again, this question can be quite simply added to the satisfaction survey for the channel. You immediately have a percentage to which you can steer, while the open answers provide insight into where there is room for improvement.

2. End-to-end improvement of the customer journey

Most unnecessary contact moments are the result of errors or ambiguities in the customer journey. The contact center itself is hardly ever the cause of the contact moments, with errors being made elsewhere in the journey. Status questions are a good concrete example of this. "What is the status of my cancellation? Have you received my application? When can I expect to receive the money in my account?" These are all signs that the information supply is unclear at various points in the customer journey, and/or that the turnaround time is overly long.

From one hundred to eight questions per week

An insurance company received many questions about the status of applications for mortality risk insurance. Following full revision of the customer journey, the new version enabled online applications to be processed within a few minutes, versus the few days required by the previous system. The questions regarding status were subsequently reduced from one hundred to only eight per week, while customers were also considerably more satisfied with the new process. A great example of a win-win situation for both customer experience and cost efficiency.

3. Online facilitation

Most large (legacy bound) service providers will not have such flashy online facilities as newer parties such as Zappos or Amazon. That is perfectly logical, when considering the complex systems required at the back. However, there is still much to be gained by facilitating – and simplifying – an online transaction process. Changes in customer details can be simply registered via a 'MyAccount'. If this can be done simply online, most customers would prefer to do so rather than having to make a telephone call.

A simple reduction of 15 percent

A bank offered an online MyAccount, which many customers only needed to use once annually for their financial statement summary. Due to such limited use of the online environment, many of them had forgotten their password by the time they needed it. In the old situation, resetting the password was a paper process requiring a telephone call from the customer. Once this had been facilitated online, it translated into a direct 15 percent reduction in contact moments. Again, these are contact moments which irritated the customer. Your organization also prefers to avoid them, as there are few opportunities to add value.

4. Proactively answering questions

Another possibility is to understand the customer so well that you can predict his questions. Smart data analyses (see chapter 6) allow you to do so relatively simply nowadays. The detailed customer journey is once again your basis, which you combine with customer contact information, plotting the timing of contact moments, number of contact moments and their content in each step of the journey. And so you know exactly when peaks can be expected and what questions will be about. Customers can then be sent an e-mail just before the peak, for example, in which you answer these questions proactively.

Proactively answering customer questions

A pilot was conducted for a healthcare insurer in order to measure the effect of proactively answering customers' questions during the healthcare campaign around October. The customer journey of the healthcare campaign is prompted by the consequences of national budget day. At that point, customers become aware of any developments concerning their healthcare in-surance. They then receive the first offer from their own healthcare insurer, by mail, in October. The data showed a peak in the contact center around three days before this offer was received. By combining this with the contact registration data, the customers' questions could be predicted. A pilot group of 60,000 customers was then sent a proactive e-mail containing answers to these questions; the remaining customers were the control group. Subse-quent analysis showed that the customers who received the e-mail were not only less likely to call than the control group, but also the actual number of customers calling was lower than in the control group. It resulted in a total of 4 to 8 percent contact reduction.

Reducing costs versus increasing value

The contact moment you avoid need not be directly translated into cost reduction and fewer employees being required. Instead, the lee-way created can be deployed to add extra value. It is however crucial to quantify this leeway in dollars. The organization is then free to invest the finance released in this manner as it chooses. There are numerous options for creating value, by proactively contacting loyal customers to make them a relevant offer, for example. Or by investing the newly released budget in more time for customer calls in order to engage them in online opportunities relevant to their situation. Take some time and you'll soon devise plenty of ideas for adding value.

5.6 Successful mobilization

Chapter 9 discusses elements which play a role in the successful im-plementation of customer signals management. However, there are two more specific elements which allow you to avoid unnecessary customer contact in such a way that this also improves results.

Time pressure

Cost reduction programs are often under time pressure. An essen-tial first step is therefore to justify the potential of reduction while identifying opportunities for improvement. You need to substantiate this, to remove the risk of time pressure catching up, and discussions developing on matters such as shorter opening hours (or other interventions), which indeed contribute to the costing target but not to improved customer experience. Effective management of that playing field is crucial. You require data to do so, translated into dollars.

Babylonian issues
In most organizations, the contact center is seen to be the problematic department. It's too expensive, therefore the number of contact moments must be reduced. However, there is little awareness that the lion's share of contact moments is not caused by the contact center itself. The other channels or the customer journey are responsible for these contact moments occurring, and many contact centers are unable to defend this argument effectively. The people of the departments playing a rol in the customer journey do not speak the contact center language, while the contact center struggles to find the right words outside their own operation. You therefore need to establish a very good relationship between all involved. If you fail to do so, you will become stranded in the discussion and will not be able to mobilize other customer journey participants to assist in the process. Facilitate translation into hard cash on the one hand therefore, but also advocate the use of the customer journey to identify the exact source of unnecessary contact.

As you know by now, customer signals management relies on the frequent use of data-based analyses. In the following chapter, we'll explain why they are so important and which commonly heard myths can be busted through the use of data.

6 DATA-DRIVEN APPROACH

Tortoises can tell you more about the road than hares.

– KAHLIL GIBRAN

Customer signals management makes frequent use of quantitative data. It is necessary in order to connect to the way in which organizations are managed, in order to mobilize people and to not get stuck in the intention to improve. There are however other reasons for a data-driven approach to the required change and improved customer experience, when underpinning facts or busting restrictive in-company myths.

6.1 Initial data check

One of the first data checks on your list is to investigate how many customers have no contact at all with your organization and also no transactions, and to identify those customers. After all, monitoring of customer journeys and channels always applies to those customers who have recently undertaken a journey or dealt with a channel. What if only 70 percent of your customers undertakes such steps within any year? This means that the other 30 percent of customers will not become happier customers when you improve the customer journey or channels. They will need something else. Therefore start by determining what percentage of customers is not in the picture in that sense. You will need to design a separate survey for them if you wish to improve total satisfaction of all customers.

6.2 Myths stagnate change

We are all customers. That means that we all know where improvements can be made in the customer experience. While you might expect this to be very advantageous, it is actually one of the greatest disadvantages when wishing to improve the customer experience within your organization. After all, we all think we know what's best for customers and we'll all do our utmost to realize that. This means that you will sometimes need to do some stubborn myth busting (along with the occasional confirmation) if you want to implement the right interventions which customers truly believe important for improved customer experience. That's where data come in.

The fifty-something manager as a source of stagnation

In an organization facing the challenge of increasing the degree of digital services available, the project manager constantly ran up against a brick wall. The source of the resistance had been unclear for some time. In the end, he started to classify the feedback received from the organization, and came to the following conclusion: the fear of transition was mainly felt among the fifty-something management echelon, who believed digitalization to be scary for customers. Of course, it is these managers themselves who feel daunted by digitalization and are unaware that customers have been placing orders online at Amazon.com for many a year and have been banking online for even longer.

I'm certainly not advocating replacing these managers... It is however a great example of how everyone in the organization thinks from their own standpoint and assumes that their ideas also apply to all customers. The required change will therefore need conscious attention from you if it is to be successful.

6.3 Busting commonly heard myths

Many organizations share common challenges. Many myths have grown on the work floor in recent years, and some of them have even been substantiated with data. Let's look at the five most common myths you will encounter and what story the data told.

Myth 1: waiting times and selection menus are the greatest irritation factors

Almost all customer service departments are driven by the so-called service level: answer as many telephone calls as possible within a certain period. This is done in the belief that the waiting time is a major irritation factor for customers, which should be avoided. However, many studies (incl. Van der Aa, 2011) have shown that a more friendly employee and receiving the right answer in one go are nearly three times as important as the waiting time. And the selection menu which is so often a cause for irritation, is even five times less important than that friendly employee who gives you the right answer the first time around. Therefore if you have 10,000 dollars to invest in improving satisfaction with telephony, it is five times better invested in increasing the rate of first time fixes and the behavior of the employees than in improving the selection menu. Of course there is a limit to the desired length of a selection menu or the time that the customer must wait. For example, waiting times mustn't run back up to those of a number of years ago, when many Internet providers could not be reached at all. However, most organizations have long since achieved a service level of 70 percent of calls answered within thirty or sixty seconds. From the customer satisfaction point of view, there is therefore little point in trying to shorten this any further. Instead, your attention would be better directed at employees and first time fixes.

Myth 2: quickly replying to e-mail has priority

Similar studies were conducted among customers to determine satisfaction with e-mail contact and what they thought most important. The majority of organizations are driven by factors such as a speedy response and the quality of the reply. But how important is the customer's perception of the employee? As in the case of telephony, the human aspect is once again crucial. At one of the organizations, this was even twice as important as the hard data such as response time and clarity of the reply. So what if this organization can invest 10,000 dollars in improving customer satisfaction with the e-mail channel?

Increasing the sense of empathy will be twice as effective as improving the response time.

In another organization, empathy was equally as important as the response time and quality of the reply. It certainly does play a role therefore, though such aspects are rarely included in customer satisfaction surveys regarding e-mail. And as you can see, the impact per organization can differ. You therefore need to ensure that you validate the driver analysis for the organization rather than simply applying driver analyses derived from other organizations.

Myth 3: customers with a MyAccount call less often
Almost every organization has a so-called 'MyAccount' nowadays: an environment into which customers log in for insight into their own details, and where they can often also directly arrange matters online. At an insurance company that wished to speed up its digital services and simultaneously reduce the number of customer contact moments, it was believed that encouragement of the MyAccount was an effective method. Analysis of the calling behavior of customers with and without MyAccount showed that customers with a type A MyAccount made less calls than customers without a type A MyAccount. This was indeed as expected. However, customers with a type B MyAccount actually made more calls than customers with no MyAccount at all. The relevance, quality and functionality of a MyAccount are all variables which play a role in the calling behavior of customers. Once again, the motto is: check what is the reality in the organization rather than accepting the standard in-company preconceptions.

Myth 4: you will receive more e-mails when steering towards online
There isn't an organization around at the moment which isn't working on further digitalization of its services. One of the stubborn myths in this sense is that steering towards the online channel results in an increase in the e-mail channel. The question is whether that is the real cause. An organization suddenly detected no less than 30 percent growth in the number of e-mails received, and immediately came to the conclusion that this was caused by increased online steering in the past year. Those parties directly involved had serious doubts however, and took a detailed look at what had happened. As in many organi-

zations, there was no overview of the many routings in the e-mail software (which e-mails with which subjects are to be internally forwarded to which departments?), so that they no longer knew which routings had been defined and why. In the end, one of these routings was found to have changed, resulting in the increased e-mail traffic. Within six months, the 30 percent increase had been converted into a 5 percent decrease, while the steering towards online continued.

While other organizations do experience increased e-mail contact, steering to online is not always the underlying cause. Much more likely is that the quality of online services does not suffice in providing customers with answers, or does not enable them to arrange matters themselves. And so they must divert to e-mail contact after all. Once again, the organization must not assume that customers are avoiding digitalization, but must instead improve the online quality. Of course there are situations in which customers most definitely prefer personal contact. You just need to ensure that you effectively question the true cause of their desire for personal contact. Don't jump to conclusions that customers are avoiding online and therefore seeking e-mail contact.

Should e-mail rest in peace?

The added value of the e-mail channel has been the subject of discussion for many years, by customers and organizations alike. This channel almost always scores poorly in customer satisfaction after all, and is a complex management challenge within the organization. With extra questions often being required to get the right answer, a telephone call or online chat is more effective and results in a better customer experience. So is it time to dispose of the e-mail channel? There are two reasons why that will not happen: firstly, organizations fear that this will increase telephone contact moments and secondly, they believe that this channel meets a customer requirement and that its demise would harm customer satisfaction.

The Linksys organization has had the courage to completely discontinue the e-mail channel. They have seen no subsequent increase in telephone contact moments, but only in self service (Dixon, 2013). A similar situation occurred at a Dutch organization which made only one change to its online customer service page: the words 'call or mail us' were replaced by 'arrange it yourself' in the page header, directly followed by the option of calling or mailing. It resulted in a direct decrease in the number of contact moments and increased customer satisfaction. The majority of customers want to arrange their own business online – at their own speed and when it suits them. The problems only begin when the quality and convenience of the self-service process lets them down. The wrong conclusion is then drawn, i.e. that customers prefer personal contact, when all they really want is for the quality of the online environment to be improved.

Myth 5: employees fear for their jobs

As soon as you undertake a contact reduction program, contact center employees play a crucial role in registering the subject of contact moments, in providing a first time fix, in steering customers towards online, et cetera. One consequence of contact reduction is generally that a smaller team of customer service employees is required, therefore potentially putting their jobs in jeopardy.

What is fascinating in this case is that the rumors propagated by departments outside customer service, regarding employees' fear for their jobs, are more troublesome than the role this actually plays among the employees in question. "Well, the quality of the logging leaves a lot to be desired, because if employees were to do it properly, they'd be putting themselves out of a job." In reality, after of course commenting on their job security, customer service employees tend to immediately offer ten ideas on how to avoid irritating contact moments for customers. They are often strongly intrinsically motivated to make things better for customers. A potential risk in this situation is that the opposition parties within the organization will have the munition to become entrenched, simply because "the customer service logs are no good". It can then take a great deal of time to adjust that attitude and even longer before they can be mobilized to make improvements.

So where lies the crux of all this? Make sure you can set the record straight from the customer's perspective. People tend to automatically think according to their own reality and perception, which is logical. However, this means that you must actively change such perceptions if you are to steer the organization towards improved customer experience. Otherwise, you run the risk of investing energy in the wrong points for improvement and failing to book results.

6.4   Preconditions for smart analyses

Generating such analyses is an extremely useful exercise for many organizations. But where does that insight come from? What minimum preconditions must be created to make the data available in your organization suitable for objective analysis?

Pragmatic start
The first main pitfall when making analyses is the quest for 100 percent accurate and complete analyses. The start is then characterized by data collection alone, with no further visible action for the rest of the organization and for the customers. It is often based on a sense of trying to remove uncertainty. Instead, why not simply start with what you already know? Do you only have complaints as a source, and no further customer registration system? Then start with complaints. What if you only have an annual customer satisfaction survey? It's a good starting point. Parallel to starting with the signals already available, you do need to work at establishing your sources of signals and their analysis.

There are many tools available nowadays with which you can very quickly ask customers' opinions on a subject. They allow you to collect customer information within a week, giving you an instant basis from which to kick off. No more waiting for all kinds of lengthy processes with data linking from IT therefore, you simply need a random sample of customers and their e-mail addresses in order to ask your questions. How satisfied are they with the application process? Or the telephony channel? Or whatever problem you want to solve.

Connect the right dots

In order to make analyses as referred to in the 5 myths described earlier, it is essential that you interconnect various sources of data. Most organizations will have a system which contains all customer data, such as their name, address, place of residence, age, how long they have been a customer, the products bought and the volume of the latter. It is often stored in a CRM system. Your next step is to link the customer contact data to this information. As long as everything registered has a unique customer number, the dots can all be connected technically. Customer satisfaction, customer contact moments and online data are the most interesting additions to the CRM data for customer signals management purposes:

- Which customers called us and what was it about?
- Which customers mailed us and what was it about?
- Which customers have a MyAccount and how do they seek contact?
- Which (types of) customers are most/least satisfied?
- And so on.

New CRM systems do not distinguish between customer data and other data, and instead combine both types. In practice however, very few companies have proven to have optimum availability of such integrated software. There's therefore a good chance that you'll have to connect your own dots.

Pareto

By recording telephony and e-mail data at the customer level, you can also directly check whether the Pareto principle applies: are 20 percent of my customers responsible for 80 percent of my telephone calls and e-mails? And if so, who are the 20 percent and why do they seek so much more contact than the rest? Whatever data you wish to collect therefore, always start by donning your 'data connection spectacles'. If you have yet to design a contact registration system, make sure it includes a field for the unique customer number.

Quantitative versus qualitative data
These types of analyses are not only ideal for busting or confirming myths, but they also provide you with a clear picture of those issues which fall short. However, you still know nothing about why they have fallen short. Let's assume that most of the telephone questions concern the status of the request for a new product. You have yet to discover why customers call so frequently on this subject, and so you need to apply qualitative methods to gain more detailed insight. You could enquire among contact center employees, and establish the detailed customer journey for the request in order to check matters such as response time, confirmations and communication with the customers.

A subtle yet particularly stubborn form of resistance
Are you regularly requested to provide more in-depth analysis? To have a closer look at customer group X, process Y or period Z? Be wary. Of course in-depth analyses are extremely useful. But they can also be a sign of quite a subtle yet stubborn form of resistance. There is no easier way of refusing to move than to say: "Maybe we should have another look at this analysis." You always need to look for the balance between really not knowing the cause – and therefore undertaking more in-depth analysis – and simply having a go, based on the insight which you already have and adjusting it if the improvement points do not have the desired effect. Your improvement points are not helping? Then you have yet to find the right cause. In other words, try some more experiments before conducting another analysis.

6.5 Measurable experiments

Even when an organization is ready to undertake such an experiment, there is still insufficient attention for how to measure its effect. What information do you require in order to determine whether the experiment can be rolled out or not? And when can we classify the experiment as a success? How important are the costs versus the customer satisfaction: are the costs allowed to increase strongly if this means customers score us a 9? Or should the costs strongly decrease if this results in customers scoring us a 6? These are all relevant questions which need to be answered beforehand, as you will otherwise have no idea what to do after the experiment.

Customer experience experiments must in any case provide measurement of an increase or decrease in:

- the customer satisfaction;
- the number of complaints;
- the number of social media posts;
- the number of customer contact moments;
- the efficiency benefit in the process (less manual processing, less double work, for example).

You can also define very specific information per experiment, on the basis of which you can take the right decision: whether or not to roll out the experiment, and how to justify your decision.

Steering towards use of the contact form

With a view to the e-mail channel proving inefficient for customers and the organization, an organization devised the idea of actively steering customers to the contact form. This notion met with great resistance within the organization, in the belief that customers would not appreciate having to complete the contact form rather than sending an open e-mail. Yet nobody actually knew whether this was the case. The only known fact was that customers were not particularly satisfied with the existing e-mail process, which they scored 6.5. Besides the less-than-perfect customer satisfaction, another reason for stimulating use of the contact form was the difficulty encountered in routing e-mails, and the resultant manual processing and double work. Better routing via the contact form saves e-mails from lying around unanswered, while customers receive quicker and better replies.

The organization monitored the following measuring information during this pilot: satisfaction with the e-mail channel, number of complaints on this subject, number of social media posts on this subject, internal improvement of routing and response time for e-mail handling. As preparation for calamities, the organization had ensured that it would always be possible to immediately revert to the former situation. Their definition of calamities encompassed either a strong increase in negative signals for customer experience or unforeseen errors in the organization's routing. All this internal fear regarding customer experience was proven to be unjust, as analyses showed that customers completing the contact form were just as satisfied as customers using the e-mail address. In fact, they were slightly more satisfied though not significantly so. Another great example of not assuming what the customer will think, but simply having a go and monitoring what happens.

We should not be afraid to experiment more, as long as the results of the experiment are measurable. Most organizations struggle to experiment however. On the one hand, this is due to the complexity of organizations and therefore their inability to act swiftly, but on the other hand also due to the deep-seated myths. People often foresee roadblocks, though nobody knows whether they are real or imagined. They do however cause congestion and delays in the process of daring to experiment. One of the ways around this which will alleviate their fears to some extent, is to provide an experiment which can be very easily reversed. Thanks to all the technical options available in today's digital environments, you can quite simply switch something 'on' and 'off' again if it proves ineffectual.

6.6 Data and emotional experience

In recent years, more and more people seem to be convinced that emotions are the only way to make leaps and bounds in customer experience: a score of 8 or more which truly leads to enhanced loyalty or trust. They also believe that improving the functional experience will never score you more than a 7, which translates as getting the basics right. You can use customer signals management to justify whether that is the case. You then see that the branch, the organization, the customer journey and the target group determine whether the emotional customer experience plays a significant role, or whether giant leaps can also be taken via the functional experience (see tips and tools 'Functional versus emotional experience').

Check the importance of emotions

The problem with emotional experience is often that it is not supported by facts. Instead, it relies on our human beliefs: of course it's nice if someone is friendly, if they proactively initiate contact or send me a bunch of flowers. And so the same will apply to our customers. Nobody looks at the actual impact of emotions. However, emotions are governed by the same rules: use data to substantiate whether that is really where you can make the difference. It can be done simply by adding emotion to the questionnaires used to formulate driver analyses, as in chapter 4: company X treated me respectfully; the employee showed great empathy; I felt the employee was listening; et cetera. These are all emotion-based statements which can be added to the questionnaire in order to determine whether the emotional experience is important for customers in that customer journey for a particular organization – and if so, in what way?

The human dimension does matter

I must of course note that emotion – and especially just the human dimension – certainly often plays an important role in satisfaction analyses. Some of you may now be thinking: so why should we bother proving it? Because you are functioning in the context of an organization faced with so many different aspects that it needs to know where energy can best be invested. All too often, these softer factors are not improved, because although everyone believes them relevant, nobody can prove their actual importance in relation to other elements of the customer journey. It takes little effort to render them measurable via driver analyses, so why miss out on such an opportunity?

TIPS & TOOLS

Functional versus emotional experience

Many a document has been written in recent years to address the question of how customers can be made so happy that they will sing your praises. Virtually all these visions are based on the emotional experience which makes the difference. But is that really the case? No, the value of emotional versus functional experience depends on the branch, customer journey and target group. And even more importantly: you no longer need to guess its value or rely on your gut feeling, but instead can simply measure it.

Case study: social services department
One of the beliefs held by a social services department was that the functional experience, and particularly the turnaround time, was extremely important in their situation. If the customer doesn't know whether she can feed her children tomorrow, it's lovely that you're so friendly but that doesn't help fulfill a primary necessity of her life. They also believed that the importance of the drivers could vary greatly between those people whose request for benefit payments had been granted and those who had been rejected. A questionnaire was therefore put to both groups of customers in order to check whether the models were indeed different. Yes, they certainly were.

Functional items mainly determine satisfaction
Elements such as turnaround time and clarity of the process were top of the list by far, among those customers whose request for benefit payments had been granted. Factors such as being treated respectfully, the sense of promises being kept, availability for questions and limited effort being required, came in third place. You can therefore make all the difference for these customers, at this stage of the customer journey (requesting benefit), by shortening the turnaround time of the request versus the statutory eight-week period.

Emotional items mainly determine satisfaction
The situation was quite the opposite for customers whose request had been rejected. Here, the emotional items were top of the list by far (being treated respectfully, the sense of promises being kept, always available for questions, et cetera). The other factors hardly mattered at all, because the emotional experience was four to six times more important than anything else.

Logical surely?
When quoting this case as an example, the standard reaction is nearly always: "Yes of course, that feels pretty logical if I was in either of those target groups." Yet organizations which approach the design of their customer satisfaction surveys from this perspective are few and far between. Instead, they tend to determine for themselves which emotions are relevant for com-

munication by the organization or the brand, never checking the value of these emotions for customers in the various steps of their journey.

An added factor is that there is little sexiness to be found in strong improvement of the functional experience. It can however really make a difference to customers, while many organizations are still somewhat lacking in this sense. Of course the situation is totally different for organizations such as KLM, Apple and Amazon when compared with a social services department, but they all need the same approach: make sure you know what is important for your customers' experience.

In other words:

1. Design your survey from the end-to-end customer journey perspective, to include both functional and emotional items.
2. Make sure you measure the value of the emotional experience per detailed journey and target group.
3. Determine which emotions your company wishes to convey and check whether they matter to customers.

And so you objectively measure what is important to your own customers, rather than everybody convincing each other of what they believe the customer wants. As an organization, you steer the improvement of your services from the customer's point of view.

6.7 Big data

Where would a modern day chapter on the importance of a data-driven approach be without saying something about big data? The million-dollar question is: what exactly is big data? When searching for recent blogs on this subject, the focus lies on the analytical possibilities of data and the significance for the marketing profession. Think in terms of being able to analyze those products most important to the customer and then offering them at that moment which gives the best chance of success (conversion). Or the A/B testing of new online application procedures. But isn't that what CRM software did some twenty years back? And what smart data analysts have been doing for years? So is big data not just a newly hyped term for an age-old challenge, namely data-driven steering of the (marketing) organization?

Just like customer engagement is a newly hyped term for something which has remained unchanged for many a year, namely: how to optimally gear your services to customer requirements?

What is certainly true, is that the volume of data is increasing exponentially. Digital developments enable us to register more and more information nowadays, and the complexity therefore increases, both commercially and technically speaking. From the commercial point of view, it is increasingly difficult to determine what data is relevant for use in which situation. You only need to think about the fact that you can nowadays pinpoint your customers' physical location. What opportunities does that offer your organization? Can people think far enough out of the box to determine its value? Technology must provide ever more sophisticated software and hardware in order to apply smart analyses to all this data. Is there anyone sufficiently versed in these techniques within your organization, to dare to make the necessary investments? This all has consequences for the competences of marketing professionals. Comprehension of data and the techniques for analysis of data are gaining importance. Yet the essence of big data is precisely the same as twenty years ago: the optimum application of information to gain even better insight into customer needs, in order to gear your products and services more effectively and thus generate extra turnover while spending your marketing budget more efficiently.

With all these insights in mind, the time is now ripe to determine your next step in improving the end-to-end customer journey, based on everything your customers tell you. In the following chapter, you'll learn how customer signals management can optimize that improvement process and how it relates to innovation.

7 IMPROVEMENT AND INNOVATION VIA CUSTOMER SIGNALS

No problem can be solved from the same level of consciousness that created it.

— ALBERT EINSTEIN

Thanks to all the insights gained from customer signals management, you can very specifically pinpoint the best potential for improvement. The challenge is then to correctly analyze the cause of the problem and to initiate a process which allows the organization to continually improve.

7.1 Lean and other methods

Many organizations work with Lean or other methods in order to improve processes. Customer signals management is also a quest for what works well and what could potentially be improved. Where lies the difference? Lean techniques are certainly useful during the phase in which you identify the cause. In practice however, the existing improvement methods are often still strongly oriented towards the internal organization. Where can we improve efficiency, where are we wasting time? The voice of the customer definitely represents the customer's interests in the Lean theory, but this customer perspective often seems to be omitted or insufficiently addressed in practice. When it comes to customer signals management, the cause analysis phase continually considers the customer's perspective of what goes wrong, as the basis from which to identify internal improvements.

7.2 The improvement process

Let's imagine that the satisfaction analyses show compliance with agreements to be an important knob to improve customer experience, and that this is not a strong point of the organization when it comes to the purchasing process. How can you identify the cause? And how can you measure the effect of your efforts?

Identifying the specific cause
There are many techniques at your fingertips in this phase, to understand the customer's problem properly. This is the phase in which qualitative techniques are your best buddy. After all, you want to know the why and wherefore.

TIPS & TOOLS

Head for the archives

An organization had a great deal of unnecessary customer contact regarding its debit process. The first step undertaken was to listen to contact center conversations in order to understand the underlying cause. It soon became apparent that some customers could not understand why a certain amount was debited, and similar types of situations were also discovered when canceling or adjusting a product. After analyzing the conversations, the detailed customer journey was established for both the cancellation and mutation processes. At the end of each process, customers received a letter stating the amount to be received or paid as a result of the cancellation or mutation. This was followed by the actual debit or credit of that amount.

The bottom line proved difficult to fathom, and one hundred archived files were therefore consulted. They were studied to determine what letters had been sent to customers and what action the financial administration department had taken. Lo and behold, there was a discrepancy between the amount stated in the letter and the actual debited or credited amount, in no less than 80 percent of the cases. All kinds of extra amounts had been added or deducted. No wonder customers felt the need to pick up the phone.

The only way of discovering such inconsistencies is to examine the end-to-end customer journey. The department sending the letters is separate to the department answering customer questions and separate again to the department collecting or repaying the money. This would never have been discovered without comparing the content of the archived letters with the financial administration data.

Detailed customer journey

Establishing a detailed customer journey is always a good place to start. If we look at the example of 'becoming a customer', you begin with the purchasing process. After that, you can zoom in on components of the purchasing process in which 'compliance with agreements' plays a role.

Customer panel

You can invite customers who have recently experienced this process, in order to get a better idea of what 'compliance with agreements' means to them. Nieuwland and Nooitgedacht (2015) compare this very effectively with a discussion of elephants: ask two people to describe an elephant and you'll end up with two very different elephants. Yet an elephant is a very tangible concept. Imagine how much more tricky it is for subjects such as 'complying with agreements' or 'treating someone respectfully'. And so it's time to talk to customers, to understand what they mean and their preferences in such matters. Only then should you take an internal look to identify what processes are not working. All too often, a solution is sought without exactly knowing why it's really necessary.

Customer arena

Another great technique is a so-called customer arena, especially if you want to make the organization even more aware of the customer's perspective. This is a session in which a conversation is conducted with a number of customers, in the center of the room. All around them are people from the organization. In the first round, they only listen to the conversation. In the second round, they may only put questions to the customers. And in the third round, without the customers, the employees discuss what they have heard and how they can apply the newfound insight.

Employee panel

Organizations often fail to take full advantage of employees and their know-how. Customer service staff can provide a wealth of signals, and therefore represent great added value in dealing with very specific problems. Ask them in more detail precisely what customers tell them about unclear invoices. They have less added value however when determining the best points for improvement at the more general level. These employees are too operational for that purpose, with insufficient insight into the end-to-end journey. Once again there is a balance to be found: using data to measure shortcomings, and then inviting employees to supplement information in qualitative sessions, in order to understand context and identify causes. In the example of the invoice, it would be interesting to compile a group to include employees from customer service, from the invoicing department and from the department which received complaints about the invoice.

Qualitative survey

When it comes to very specific issues, a questionnaire can be put to a number of customers to determine their thoughts on the theme. Avoid using statements in this case, instead posing more open questions on the subject. Imagine you want better understanding of how online declarations can be simplified. For a health care insurer wanting to improve the online experience, you could ask questions such as:

- Which organization do you think has simple online services?
- Can you indicate why you find them simple?
- What moments in time best suit you to submit healthcare declarations?
- What moments in time best suit you to submit them online?
- Which organization do you think has awful online services?
- Can you indicate why you find them awful?
- What are the main thresholds for you when arranging matters yourself online?
- Can you give three examples which for you represent extremely simple services, outside the insurance branch?

Take care that the questions do not become too trivial or direct. Try to include as much context as possible, in order to trigger customers to share more insights than they themselves might initially have imagined.

This list of ideas is certainly not exhaustive. The purpose of the exercise is to become aware of the importance of using such techniques and of the timing with which they are deployed. Make sure you stay up to date with the latest creative techniques therefore – both online and off line – so that you can apply not only effective but also energizing and inspiring methods to make the rest of the organization enthusiastic.

Monitoring the effect
Once you have clarity on the actual cause, it's time to put the improvement points in motion. In this phase, organizations often fail to truly monitor the effects of their efforts and whether or not the efforts have had the required results. Many a business case has been drawn up, for example, without subsequently checking whether it has indeed been implemented as designed. And even if the effect is measured, it is more likely to be organization-centric than customer-centric. Have we saved time? Do we need less people? Yet the effect from the customer's perspective is very simply measurable nowadays, thanks to all the available tooling for continuous monitoring. Make sure you add a number of smart questions to the existing surveys, or design a separate baseline survey with follow-ups for the specific improvement point.

Cause and consequences
Let's imagine you see increased satisfaction with a certain customer process. It's very difficult to specify exactly what caused the increase. Don't get bogged down with wanting to know the details down to the last decimal point. In reality after all, ceteris paribus does not exist (the notion that all other things remain equal, except that one element which you have changed). Multiple factors always occur simultaneously, which can influence customers' experience. By regularly meeting and discussing the effects, and whether or not actions have been

implemented, you will gain more and more insight into effective and ineffective interventions. And even more importantly: internal enthusiasm will be boosted when employees recognize the effect of their efforts directly from the customer's reaction. This will motivate them to continue the list of improvements.

7.3   Organization of continuous improvement

As an organization, you do not want the aforementioned steps to be a one-off occurrence, but preferably a process of continuous improvement of your services. Customer signals management does so by working in so-called customer journey teams.

Customer journey teams
The workshops for establishment of the end-to-end customer journey are intended for everyone who plays a role in the journey from the customer perspective. You will forge this group of people into a customer journey team responsible for continuous improvement of the customer journey elements under their control. Together with them, you will design a cycle which begins with facilitation of insights and ends with feedback of the measured results and selection of the following points for improvement.

This will generally be virgin territory for the members of the customer journey team. While they may already have some experience with learning circles or Lean, they will not have encountered analyses of all insights offered by customer signals and own responsibility for the total process of improving services. It is therefore essential that these teams are facilitated by those persons responsible for customer signals management within the organization, especially in the beginning. Facilitation means: providing insights, but also tips and tools.

Facilitation through insights
Insights can be manifold. What you're doing here is combining all your customer insights of the journey in question and applying a first round of analysis. What are the most important points of the satisfaction survey? What are the most important knobs to turn? What are

the most commonly heard complaints? The most commonly occurring questions by telephone and e-mail? Why do customers visit our offices? Where do customers get stuck online when arranging matters themselves? Generate an overview of these insights and involve the customer journey team in order that you all share common knowledge, and that you can interpret the information correctly and jointly identify the desired improvement areas.

Facilitation through tips and tools
The next groundbreaker is to do something with these improvement areas. Not the actual improvement process, but rather how the customer's perspective helps you discover why things are going wrong. Teach the team members to define their own detailed journey, how to collect recordings of telephone calls, take random samples of letters or e-mails, and so on. Help them on their way with tips and tools to identify the appropriate improvements in their department.

Number of customer journey teams
Take a close look at the number of customer journey teams. In the example of the main ten-step journey of an insurance company, ten teams were not required. The choice fell upon a customer journey team per product group (healthcare and non-life), each one therefore encompassing marketing, online, customer service, back office, finance and IT. In this organization, the data showed only 10 percent of customers to purchase both non-life and health care products. The team compilation was therefore ideal in their case.

All kinds of factors influence the compilation of the teams. We suggest you start by making pragmatic choices, forming a single team and discovering what works and what not, as you go along. Experiment and learn, don't spend a year devising how best to compile your teams in order to optimally serve the interests of customers and the organization. As soon as you see results stagnating, you can always head back to the drawing board to redefine a more effective team. The process should not be cast in concrete, but rather organically growing.

Keep people on board
Enthusiasm is the most important 'knob' you, as the process supervisor, can turn. So give some conscious thought to how you can render the customer journey team enthusiastic and keep them that way. Take the team members to other organizations, have them talk to customers, use film clips and other inspiring methods to refresh their minds and remind them of the importance of customer-centric reasoning.

7.4 Embedding the new method

Experience has shown these types of processes to require at least a year in order to become embedded. Until then, it's sensible not to loosen the reins. If the customer journey teams are to gradually gain a sense of responsibility for the improvement process, it's important that you pay this attention right from the start. The risk otherwise is that everyone looks to the person coaching the process, awaiting his example before initiating any own action. Make sure the sessions therefore always include time for the discussion required to encourage their autonomous approach, so that the coaches can gradually step back out of the limelight and eventually walk out the door.

Management role
The dialog which always unfolds – generally even in the first session – goes like this: "These teams are a great initiative, because we never really work together enough. And our organization really needs to focus on how customers think. But we're already so busy, and now this is extra work as well, I wonder whether the management will support us." Although caution is always advised when employees tend to await and expect a management response, they do have a point. After all, not many organizations work according to Google-type principles of fully autonomous, well-educated professionals. On the contrary, you are often confronted with organizations in which hierarchic functioning is the norm. In that case, you may well want everybody to be spontaneously autonomous, but this is neither realistic nor fair. You can of course take steps in that direction, but that will require more than simply customer signals management. We are then talking total cultural change.

As soon as the hierarchy comes into play, you must take it seriously in the customer signals management approach. In concrete terms, this means that the superiors of team members, and the management echelon to whom they in turn answer, must all be made to recognize the importance of working in customer journey teams. They too must be facilitated, by clearly envisaging the benefits of working in customer journey teams. Have them discuss the process in departmental meetings, in monthly newsletters, in presentations, et cetera. Ensure that they are actively involved in advocating the importance of this new initiative and have them regularly share their experience of successful aspects, but also of less noteworthy initiatives. After all, this needs to be a process of continuous learning and improvement.

Coaching role
The team coaches must also make an effort, in order that the employees are lovingly and fairly reflected in everything they do, thus removing any cause for martyrdom. All too often, employees will otherwise continue to point a finger at the management, or at anyone except themselves. Yes, it is the management's role to afford them space and not to be swayed by the issues of the day, but it is the employees' responsibility to undertake action and to call to account anybody who does not comply with the agreements. Once the team is firmly established and the management has adopted the importance of customer journey teams, the coaches can gradually retire. The latter will always play a role when gathering insights, as this should not be left to the teams themselves. With the exception of this analysis of insights, the teams should certainly be capable of implementing the process, as long as they are given a sufficiently loose rein to do so.

Aim for connection
Connection is an essential factor in customer signals management. You are not only connecting departments within the end-to-end journey, and the organization with the customer, but also connecting employees and management. In virtually all organizations, the management will point the finger at employees, and vice versa, when it comes to improving services from the customer's perspective. Don't be tempted to join in, instead focus on making the connections between

all parties. The customer is the objective means for that purpose, who tells the organization exactly what can and must be improved.

Reporting line to MT and board

In order to implement and embed the improvement process throughout the organization, it is essential to include the MT and the board in the progress, and to mobilize them where necessary. People are often hesitant to call in the assistance of the MT when necessary, as it feels like escalation. These are personal preconceptions, which are often unfounded. You are in fact serving the process optimally if you do not monopolize all the improvement points, but rather provide insight into the situation, take everyone's role seriously and sometimes simply let things happen. Facilitate the process, communicate what is required to improve it and encourage everyone to adopt their role for successful improvement of the services (see also chapter 9).

7.5 From improvement to innovation

Customer signals nearly always show that there are still so many gains to be made when getting the basics right that you more likely require improvement processes rather than complete innovation of services. After all, from the customer signals management perspective, getting the basics right also translates into that proactive advice, that listening ear, the bunch of flowers when necessary. And there's more to this process than meets the eye. However, many organizations also feel the need for more innovative approaches, thinking out of the box together with customers in order to design new services. Customer signals management is then certainly an effective place to start. In order to raise the innovation bar even further, you can then look at two adjacent methods which can play an important role in innovation.

The ideal customer journey

A really effective method is to combine establishment of the existing end-to-end customer journey and the out-of-the-box vision of how it could be. By first establishing the existing journey, you not only raise awareness of what it means to think from the customer's perspective among organization members, but also directly alert them to anomalies in the process, which require improvement. If the team is informed beforehand of all insights from the signals, they will have empathy for the customer and his needs. With that as the basis, the team members can establish the ideal customer journey. This ideal can then be checked among customers and fine tuned into a new service or new process which benefits both the customer and the organization.

These types of sessions are not suitable for everyone. Choose carefully which type of people are to work on the ideal in each phase. It is often useful to divide this into two steps: firstly a team which can pour its soul into the ideal situation, and secondly a number of realists who take a critical look at what is feasible and what not. Thus a number of iterations will give you an implementable plan. All too often, the vision is either so far out of the box (and unrealistic) that it disappears into a drawer, or it is so realistic that the group loses all sense of innovation and the energy ebbs away. Make sure the session includes a number of doers, who take concrete action after the session in order that the plan is actually implemented.

Service design

If you truly want to innovate from a 100 percent customer perspective, service design is a fantastic method, which was developed (among others) at the University of Delft on the basis of industrial design techniques. Based on the context mapping technique*, it takes a qualitative view of the context of people, their customer experience and their latent needs, but without the limitations of the organization. By actually fathoming the context and needs of people, you can then develop new concepts which serve the interests of both the organization and the customer. Combining these qualitative insights with quantitative data in customer signals management, gives you the perfect basis for innovation.

---

* Developed by Dr. Froukje Sleeswijk Visser, see also contextmapping.com and www.muzus.nl/en.

Application in practice
Many social services departments face the issue of what is required to get people off supplementary benefit. This is not only in the interests of the social services but also beneficial for the customer. After all, most people simply want to work. Many interventions have already been tried, but have not yet had the desired results. Service design allows you to look very specifically at the context and world experienced by these people, in order to gain insights which lead to much more effective solutions than those already devised. These always take account of the win-win situation of customers and organizations.

Chapter 8 follows on from this by focusing on the internal organization and the role played by employees in all facets of customer signals management.

8 WHAT ROLE DO EMPLOYEES PLAY?

Concentrate on the person pouring your wine, for he is of importance and not the cup.

— JALAL AL DIN RUMI

Customers are key in customer signals management. But what role do employees play? Employee satisfaction certainly has an impact on customer experience. And how about the customer centricity of the employees? Does the image held by management match that held by the customer?

8.1 Perception of employees

Employees play an important role in virtually all driver analyses for customer satisfaction, and the friendliness of employees is almost always a factor. The mismatch lies in the management perception in organizations looking to increase their customer centricity. Managers almost always claim that employees need to be more customer centric. Yet if you look at the scores in all the surveys, few elements score as highly as appreciation of the employee. Generally speaking, the employees do not need training in customer centricity, though of course there are organizations which form the exception to this rule. However, the benefits to be gained nearly always concern conversational skills rather than intrinsic customer centricity.

Employees who are in contact with customers tend to consciously choose this work, and they do indeed score extremely high on the scale of intrinsic customer centricity. It is more of a problem that employees struggle to look beyond their own task and department in order to improve the total services provided to the customer. This has nothing to do with a lack of training, but rather with the way in which the organization is set up and the departments managed. As an invoicing employee, if I'm only ever requested to produce a good run and never to consider the end-to-end journey from the customer's point of view, it's hardly fair to accuse me of not being customer centric enough. Organizations would do well to first consider this when wondering why so few improvements are made in the end-to-end customer journey. Employees take their work very seriously and have good reason to do what they do. Appreciate that and ask them in detail about the reasons behind their actions. This will help you discover core issues and their perspective, for inclusion in your desired innovation process.

Focus on the actual cause

A chemist wishes the service employees to pay more attention to the so-called duty of care questions (are you familiar with the side-effects? Do you know how the medication should be taken? etc.), along with a friendly attitude to customers. They are looking for training options for this purpose. Once again, they head straight for a solution without taking a good look at the underlying cause. The management was shown not to spend any attention on either point in their interaction with employees. There was no discussion of the matter, and their behavior was not corrected. A training course for the employees will have little point if you do not first address the management (or at least parallel to the training), in order that they too pay attention to the two themes. As an organization, you steer your own direction. You therefore need to make conscious choices on how to steer employees and departments.

8.2   Various blood groups

Because customer signals management looks at the end-to-end journey from the customer's perspective, you are dealing with three blood groups:

1. employees with customer contact;
2. employees without customer contact;
3. employees in a staff position.

Very different themes apply in these three groups.

1. Employees with customer contact

The people who choose this profession are all intrinsically motivated to help customers. It is what gets them out of bed each morning. They work in a context in which they are confronted daily with those elements of the customer services which go wrong. They often feel their voice goes unheard when it comes to points where services can be improved. "We've told them so often but nothing ever happens" is a commonly heard and often justified complaint. This applies both to contact center employees and to employees in roles such as case manager or customer manager in the front office of an organization, who man the service desk for example. They have little empathy with staff employees ("they have no idea how it works in practice") and employees without customer contact ("surely you can just call the customer yourself and help him?").

2. Employees without customer contact

The people who consciously choose a department which does not have contact with customers – think in terms of an invoicing department or administrative back office – do so for a good reason. They feel a great barrier between themselves and the customer and are not good at customer contact. This should not be required of them. They process files and often wear internal spectacles, paying special attention to guarding against errors in rules and procedures. They too believe the staff employees to be too far removed from the practical situation, but for other reasons than the customer contact employees. And in their view, the customer contact employees are too lenient in complying with customers' wishes, with all the resultant risks such as non-compliance with procedures, fraud, et cetera.

3. Employees in a staff position

The people who consciously opt for a staff position – i.e. not directly in the primary process; think in terms of policy or also marketing – are mainly distanced from the customer. They do not have direct customer contact, nor are they dealing with customer files on a daily basis. They are often well-educated professionals, who have little empathy with the other two types of employees. In practice, for example, marketing people rarely visit the contact center and policymakers struggle to connect with practical execution levels.

Connection

So how will you interconnect these three groups? Because you will need that connection if you are to optimize services in the end-to-end journey. The great thing is that you feel the energy in all three groups when improving the total services for customers. The customer is objective and binding, allowing you to bring them together. This type of session in which you establish a detailed customer journey for example, can also create empathy with each other. They do not otherwise have much contact, and therefore no idea of each other's work and reasons behind certain matters. That's the first thing you hear: "It's great to finally know what Pete from department X really does, I had no idea. We should do this more often." You therefore need to be aware of the differences between these three blood groups and the wariness between them. That wariness is mainly due to them not knowing each other. It is hard to feel connection with an abstract department X which often causes problems in your own work, while it's nice to connect with Pete of the same department X, whom you can now call or e-mail if there are issues.

Unconscious miscommunication

An organization employed two complaints coordinators. A new team leader was subsequently recruited, who was to work with the two coordinators to improve complaints management. This organization comprised a number of brands and a number of divisions. Slowly but surely, the spaghetti of all those involved with complaints, became further unraveled. It took six months to discover that the complaints coordinators did not coordinate all complaints, and that they actually only had responsibility for 1 percent of all complaints received by the organization. There were other coordinators in other divisions for other brands for all other complaints.

Once again, we can recognize the importance of describing the elephants. The team leader implicitly assumed that they would coordinate all complaints, while it was perfectly normal for both coordinators that their scope only covered that 1 percent – that's how it had been for years.

Connection at the management level

If the end-to-end journey requires improvement, there must actually be room to do so. It must not become an ad hoc and incidental workshop, but rather the employees must be actively stimulated to continually look at the services and identify where improvements can be made in the journey. In practice, you often encounter a conflicting image at the management and board level on the one hand and the team leaders level on the other. The management feels that employees have been afforded all the room they need for improvement, while the team leaders feel that they cannot give any room at all, due to the constant management pressure regarding the daily production deadlines to be met.

The truth will be found somewhere in the middle and is actually not that significant. Much more significant is that this mechanism is encountered in many organizations. It is therefore important to create connection not only between various blood groups of employees but also between the various management echelons. What many people underestimate is that most employees were never selected for continuous improvement, for improvement of their own services or for thinking outside of their own box. In the same way that employees cannot be blamed for their lack of customer centricity, it is equally unfair to blame them for a lack of proactivity and initiative for improvement. If you steer firmly from above and keep control of the reins, you must also act firmly to give employees the room and coaching required to adjust their perspective. If they have failed to initiate their own improvements after six months or a year, then yes, you certainly can call them to account.

What is crucial to keep in mind is that you always seek connection and are not tempted to play the blaming game, as that will always result in alienation. Also important is that you keep this in mind at all levels.

8.3   Sharing customer insights

Besides establishing the customer journey together, the sharing and interpreting of the insights gained from customer signals is another great way of connecting the various people within the organization. In a sample case concerning the application for debt management, we can explain how to go about this type of session.

Collecting signals

You begin by designing a customer satisfaction survey based on the detailed customer journey. This is then subjected to a driver analysis in order to determine the knobs to turn (see chapter 4). The results of this satisfaction survey are supplemented with the most common subjects from calls, e-mails, complaints, visits and other relevant sources for signals received from customers.

Sharing the analysis

In the analysis, you check whether the insights gained from the customer satisfaction survey match the insights derived from the other signals. In this case, the contents of the plan of approach (advice) and the speed played the greatest role in the survey. This was also confirmed by the e-mails (requesting status) and the complaints (takes too long). In preparation, you list the top 3 points for improvement and introduce the group to the analysis process. In this type of session, make sure you focus on releasing energy, which works very well if you also share the positive results. Check what percentage of the customers awarded 8 or more points. An average score of 7.2 often means many customers have scored you an 8 or more. That exceeds employees' expectations, which is good for the energy level during the session. Also inform them of the percentage of customers scoring a 5 or less, which is often much lower than they would expect. Pay special attention to open answers and choose a striking example to include on the front page of the report. Then generate an overview of the positive and negative answers. The analysis is a fair representation of the reality, but you can make the difference in the way in which you link that reality to the organization.

Interpreting the analysis

It's now time for a dialog on these three themes. Are they recognizable or not? What do they represent? What image do you have when standing in the customer's shoes? Those people with customer contact can fulfill this role perfectly in the session, while the other roles know the precise pitfalls which can make a process too long, for example. Together, they are all very capable of interpreting the insights in order to arrive at a shared picture of the situation.

Devising points for improvement

This means that they are also able to formulate the points for improvement. In this phase, it is important to challenge the group effectively in two elements: thinking from the customer's point of view and avoiding thinking in impossibilities. Many internal frustrations may surface here, which will not always concern customer services. Give them the assignment: devise a maximum of five improvement points which will boost the average customer satisfaction score by half a point within three months. This will challenge them not to reduce the response time from two weeks to 10 days, but rather to think about what is needed to have that advice available within a day. Have everyone brainstorm freely on the improvement points, write them down and conclude by prioritizing them in terms of the degree of their impact on one, two or all three areas for improvement. And so you will define five definite points of improvement for which employees can take direct action.

Opening and closing the session

As soon as everyone is present, it is important to spend a moment to check whether they are all settled. Everyone is busy busy busy, running back and forth from one meeting to another. Ask whether they all have the peace of mind to be here now, or whether there is anything distracting them. This can easily be done during the introductions round, for example. When closing, one of the pitfalls is to conclude with the list of five points of improvement. Instead, take the time to render the process even more definite: who will undertake which steps at each point of improvement, and when?

8.4   Employee satisfaction

What role does employee satisfaction play in all this? As described in chapter 1, there is a relation between the satisfaction and loyalty of employees and that of customers. Yet there is still little attention for employee satisfaction, which is in the shadow previously occupied by customer satisfaction surveys some ten years ago. While all organizations have an employee satisfaction survey, it is often conducted out of a sense of obligation rather than the intrinsic drive to also really understand what matters to employees. Of course every manager and his team do their best to make it work, but the employee satisfaction theme simply does not have sufficient attention within organizations.

Employee commitment
The early 20th century saw the development of the Taylor approach: fragmenting all employee tasks where possible, to achieve maximum efficiency. After all, it was assumed that employees' only motivation was their salary. By the beginning of the 1960s, Herzberg (1966) proved that many more factors played a role and that salary was but a hygiene factor, which has also recently been confirmed within the context of employee satisfaction in the contact center (Van der Aa, 2011). So which knobs can you turn here, as you would for customer satisfaction? What you're really looking for is intrinsic drive and commitment to help improve the organization. A concurrent theme which is also part of the most important employee satisfaction knob is that of meaning: how useful do I feel at work? (Van der Aa, 2011)

Customer signals management plays an active role in this, because you are bringing the customer in from outside. We all want to feel like we matter. However because of current day trends, the fragmentation of work, the working pressure and many other reasons, we have lost sight of the meaning of our work. There are two sides to this:

1. "I don't understand why I need to do what I do."
   Within my own tasks and responsibilities, I don't understand why
   we do the things we do.
2. "I don't understand my role in the rationale of the organization."
   Because I'm only doing my own little thing, I've lost the connection
   with the bigger whole. I'm not sure why we as an organization exist
   and what my role is.

Because you are discussing the quality of customer services and
everybody's role in those services, from the customer's point of view,
you can pay attention to both points. After all, the customer is often
the link to the rationale of the organization. Reviewing this from the
customer journey perspective helps clarify the role of each employee
in this journey. And because you are considering why everyone does
what they do from the customer's point of view, you also gain insight
into people's own tasks and the degree of added value for customers.

TIPS & TOOLS

Quick insight into what matters

A manager starts in her new position in charge of the contact center. There is
great dissatisfaction among the employees and many matters which require
improvement from an operational point of view. One issue she tackles is to
ask all contact center employees three questions:
1. What should we stop doing right now?
2. What should we start doing right now?
3. What should we continue doing right now?

One of the most valuable interventions is a fortnightly meeting with the manager of the IT department, an information manager and herself. And so the
parties come together who can take immediate decisions on budget availability and whether the required solution is also commercially feasible. There
is periodical feedback with the employees on the actions to be taken. This
not only results in extremely valuable improvements for better performance
and happier customers, but also the employees are very appreciative. It takes
little effort, to give great satisfaction.

8.5   The 'knobs' of employee satisfaction

As described above, employee satisfaction certainly counts for the customer experience. As in customer satisfaction, the question once again arises: what are the most important knobs to turn for satisfied employees in your own organization?

Complex situation

It's important to realize that employee satisfaction is a much more complex phenomenon than customer satisfaction. A meta-analysis of employee satisfaction surveys (Van der Aa, 2011) showed there to be no less than 29 different factors which play a role. A few of these factors include: development opportunities, the employee's superior, the work itself, the organization, the atmosphere, learning organization, appreciation, salary, autonomy, clarity of tasks, conflicting tasks, variation, meaning. Within the context of the contact center, you can also add: learning from customers, learning from employees, organization integrity and the sharing of information between departments.

A score but no drivers

As in customer satisfaction surveys, organizations do indeed measure the satisfaction of their employees but have no idea which knobs are most important. Information provided by the management is a commonly quoted item. But if you compare this with the fact that customers almost always name the selection menu in a telephony survey, which hardly matters at all, it is questionable whether information supply actually matters.

Step-by-step plan for drivers

Driver analyses are equally important for employee satisfaction, with measurement more frequent than once every year or two years. The steps to be taken are comparable with those of the customer satisfaction survey (as described in chapter 4). Only the first step differs.

Step 1 – Qualitative sessions
The customer satisfaction survey uses the customer journey, which is not applicable in the case of employees. You could look at the HR

cycle – which must certainly be included – but a different approach is required for employees, in which you start with qualitative sessions. Depending on the number of different positions in the organization, you organize one or more qualitative sessions with employees. You need only ask two questions during the session:
1. What do you really like about your work?
2. What do you not like about your work?

Have everyone write their answers on post-its. Now generate a questionnaire based on this list of items, in order to check which points actually matter.

Step 2 – Conducting the questionnaire
The employees can now complete the questionnaire formulated on the basis of the qualitative sessions. If you are to get a good response, it's crucial that employees feel their input matters. There will often be a history of surveys which have had no follow-up. You will therefore need to pay attention to this negative 1-0 score when undertaking a new survey which you want to implement seriously. Explain carefully why this survey is unlike others, why it will be done differently and exactly what form it will take.

Step 3 – Driver analysis
The analysis for employee satisfaction is exactly the same as that for the customers. Here too, it will result in factors with an impact score. You will then know what percentage of employee satisfaction can be influenced using the measured elements.

The subconscious knobs of employee satisfaction

A survey among contact center employees has shown this method of developing questionnaires to result in the right 'knobs'. Alongside the commonly quoted elements that play a role in employee satisfaction, customer signals management elements were also important: learning from customers, learning from employees, organization integrity (including being honest with customers and the customer-centricity of the organization) and the sharing of information. The most important knob was 'development and challenge'.

It concerned three items: sufficient development opportunities within the organization; the sense that the work is meaningful; sufficient challenges at work. In terms of being meaningful, customer centricity involves many challenges and opportunities. The salary was shown to have little impact at all, which is in keeping with the hygiene philosophy that the salary only plays a role when other issues are unsatisfactory. If you do not feel your work to be meaningful, your salary suddenly becomes significant. Once again, you see the importance of objectively determining the latent knobs. While the salary is soon mentioned in the sessions, quantitative analysis shows it to pale in comparison with the importance of other knobs.

Step 4 – Improvement and continuous measurement
It very rarely occurs that employee satisfaction is measured more frequently than once per year or once per two years. But why would you not do so if you really want to see the actual effect of your efforts? More frequent monitoring in itself also impacts the employee experience when it comes to the importance of their input. It also allows you to monitor whether your interventions have had the required effect, monthly or quarterly, and to immediately adjust them as required. The other great benefit of continuous measurement is that peaks become visible. Let's imagine that a reorganization has been announced or the organization has received bad publicity, you can immediately check whether satisfaction dips in that month. And so you can once again bust many myths and prove them to be untrue.

As you have read so far, customer signals management is a very worthwhile, complex puzzle with many facets. The following chapter discusses various success factors which play a role in not only successfully introducing customer signals management but also keeping it alive and allowing it to prosper.

9
HOW TO BOOK SUCCESS IN CUSTOMER SIGNALS MANAGEMENT

A target is a dream with a deadline.

— PETER DARBO

The target of the customer signals management method is to increase the customer centricity of the organization, with measurable results. In order to do so successfully, you need to be able to take action at various levels and to know how to mobilize the organization at those levels. There is a difference between the introduction phase of customer signals management, and keeping it alive and allowing it to prosper. Another difference can be found between the management and board role and your own role.

9.1 How to bring customer signals management to life?

You aim to introduce customer signals management within the organization. You will then need to take account of seven areas of attention.

1. Connect to the organization targets
Make sure customer signals management connects to the targets of the organization at this moment. Do they concern customer retention, cost reduction, improved customer experience? And so on. Customer signals management contributes to each of these targets. It is therefore an approach that you choose and that also has consequences for the way in which you introduce customer signals management.

2. Find yourself a sponsor

People in the customer experience field often claim they require support from the management or board. That is only partly true. What is true, however, is that someone must grant you the freedom to undertake customer signals management. Nothing more, nothing less. The task of convincing all those involved of the benefits to be gained by customer signals management lies with the person wishing to implement it. By proving that it gives measurable results.

3. Be as concrete as possible

That proof also requires you to render the gains of customer signals management very concrete and tangible. Either in the cost savings which will be achieved, by avoiding unnecessary customer contact for example. Or in the experience, thanks to you clearly identifying which knobs have the most impact on customer satisfaction. And subsequently by not formulating points for improvement at the 'information and communication needs to be better' level, but rather very specifically: 'the response time of process X must be shortened' or 'the letter in step X of the customer journey must be clearer'.

4. Put on your cost-efficiency spectacles

By now, you know that cost efficiency is by no means a dirty word in customer signals management. So put on those spectacles in all the plans you make. Besides avoiding unnecessary customer contact, cost reductions can also be achieved via the digitalization process desired by customers, for example. Once the customer can arrange certain matters himself, employees have more time to do other, value adding, work.

5. Keep it small

Start with a customer process, with a channel, with a project which you can prove works. The people you need to convince have no idea what customer signals management is. There is no point requesting an internal go for 'customer signals management'. Instead, you request a go to solve a recognizable problem, using customer signals management as the method.

6. Facilitate everybody

Make sure those people you need in this process are optimally facilitated: starting with data, figures, measurements which help them realize their targets, but subsequently also with methods such as the establishment of the customer journey with the team. Teach them and coach them, and wait until a later stage to steer towards their autonomous action and embedding in the line organization.

7. Take people by the hand

Take those involved by the hand, step by step. Focus on their agenda, their top 3, the points for improvement relevant to them and ask yourself what the team needs in order to put the insights into action. Regularly check whether they still need your assistance.

9.2 How to keep customer signals management alive?

Most people will be enthusiastic to start with, because it's new and fun. Their attention will ebb after a while and you'll need to do your best to keep it alive. In this phase too, there are seven areas of attention.

1. Spread the word

In the first year, and possibly also in year two, you need people who will consistently spread the word. Who keep putting the customer on the agenda in a fun way. Make sure you're not seen as 'the customer experience nag' but rather the person who gets everyone on board.

2. Roll it out

Start with a single process, channel or project. Create enthusiasm and use this to slowly roll out customer signals management into other processes, channels and projects, to more departments, divisions and brands. In doing so, you will create a pull instead of a push strategy.

3. Embed it in the organization

After the first year, you need to ensure that your proven results have demonstrated sufficient value that the customer signals management process is no longer seen as a project but rather an ongoing element. This means that you create a new role, a person responsible for analysis of customer signals management and feeding of the organization. It also requires the development of a process in which the organization itself applies the insights and is called to account by the board when necessary.

4. Show understanding for other priorities

Assume that you will regularly have dialogs in which priorities other than customer experience become obvious, and accept this without becoming demotivated or even cynical. Your main pitfall is to believe that everyone else can make more effort, requiring you to continually communicate that. Their involvement in other priorities should not be interpreted as unwillingness, as an organization will always have multiple interests, after all. Your challenge lies in discovering the right seduction techniques to convince them to always make time for customer experience.

5. Stay creative

Always keep looking for new and creative ways of applying customer signals management. Introduce new techniques to get other people on board. Take them with you to other organizations. Continue to innovate yourself in order to keep their enthusiasm alive.

6. Share results

People need to be convinced of the added value of customer signals management. Regularly share your results therefore. It's not just all about proving that satisfaction levels have improved. Being able to show a driver analysis and naming the knobs to be turned, is an extremely valuable result in itself, to re-energize people and tangibly show what it can mean for them.

7. Know yourself

Initiating customer signals management requires other skills than its further development and embedding in the organization. Recognize your strengths and do not be afraid to call in other people in a phase where they have more added value than yourself. Be aware that you will always be paddling upstream and that you need to embrace the challenge rather than burning out.

9.3 What role is played by management and the board?

You can easily introduce customer signals management with the support of that one sponsor to invest your time in it. After the initial start-up and having demonstrated the first results, the management and board must adopt their role in embedding it in the organization. Seven areas of attention apply to them.

1. Select the right person.

In the ideal situation, you choose someone with energy and drive, and the appropriate contextual background. This has proven to be a tricky combination. If forced to choose between the two, pick the person with the right energy and drive, who is popular within the organization or sensitive enough to adjust to everyone required. While you can teach someone the content of customer signals management, intrinsic drive cannot be taught.

2. Facilitate the right know-how

The person who is to undertake customer signals management, must be able to convince many people of the method and of the importance of customer experience. This person must therefore be aware of situations and of the interests of the dialog partners, in order to attain optimal gearing. They should therefore be regularly included in matters occurring at the management and board levels.

3. Be aware of your own role

Sponsors regularly underestimate the importance of their own role in putting the importance of customer experience on the organizational map. Everyone understands that it cannot always be top of the list. Sales, costs, HR, they all require time and attention. However, always be honest about priorities towards the people working with customer experience. It is demotivating if a sponsor says yes and means no. It is better to explain that it currently has no priority and to indicate when it will be back on the agenda.

4. Watch out for energy leaks

Keep a watchful eye on whether the persons involved are not suffering from energy leaks. They are involved in a process in which they regularly run up against brick walls. A listening ear is then welcome in order to share frustrations before moving forward again, re-energized.

5. Actively ask whether assistance is required

People involved with customer experience in project form, often underestimate the importance of the formal organization. It is effective, in organizations, if one director informs another that he or she should spend some time on a subject. Therefore regularly ask whether you can do anything to help people, as their sponsor.

6. Delegate responsibilities

The project leader or the project team are aware of their responsibilities in initiating customer signals management. However, the project team cannot be made responsible for embedding the method in the organization. The choices to be made here are management and board decisions. The project group can of course provide support in their realization, but must not be concerned with the time and space for embedding in the departments.

7. Share successes

As a sponsor, you have regular contact with fellow managers or directors. Make sure you also discuss interim results and successes with them, helping to create enthusiasm for customer experience throughout the organization. Equally important is that such insights are shared with external stakeholders such as client councils, administrators and supervisory bodies.

9.4 What is the effect on your own role?

If you take up the gauntlet and accept the challenge of implementing customer signals management in the organization, that takes an effort by you personally. Here are nine tips to make the most of yourself in the role required of you.

1. Connect to other people's targets

You will have many dialog partners whom you need to keep on board in order to improve customer experience. Focus on them whenever possible. Identify their targets and connect to them, in order to realize the targets of improved customer experience.

2. Don't be right, but prove you're right

It's easy enough to keep yelling that things can be done better from the customer's perspective. That doesn't help. There's a big difference between being right and proving yourself right. Consider other people's contexts and show understanding if customer experience is not always top of their list.

3. Boil it all down

Customer experience is a fantastic field, but it can easily become a minefield of woolliness. Even the definition of 'customer journey' can be confusing enough. Reduce it all to make it as concrete and tangible as possible, without too much analysis, text and pictures to bulk things up.

4. Focus your energy on movement

All the previous chapters have taught you the importance of having the right steering facts and figures to mobilize the organization. Yet 80 percent of your work is still to get people into action, to understand what moves others. They won't just spring into action because satisfaction is sub-optimal. Show genuine curiosity for what moves people and try to avoid being judgmental.

5. Go with the flow

Many roads lead to Rome, and you will need to walk every one of them. Don't be too rigid in the route and speed with which you want to reach Rome. In the end however, make sure you actually get to Rome and not Moscow.

6. Serve the process

There are multiple interests in every organization. You need to be confident enough to communicate fairly and lovingly what you see happening around you. Serve the process instead of serving individual interests. Focus on what benefits the organization.

7. Avoid martyrdom

Many customer experience specialists claim that organizations have no time for customer experience. Take care not to become a martyr. If they have no time for you, there is either a very good reason, or you have yet to discover the right seduction method. Avoid 'we-they' stand-offs and stay connected with all those involved, to book results together. Connection does not require you to run from confrontations or become a one-man peacekeeping force. Confronting those aspects in the process which are not working well is yet another way of serving the process.

8. Practice what you preach

If you believe the organization should react to customers within 24 hours, make sure you yourself react to e-mails within 24 hours. Keep your word, reward people, send them flowers when they've earned them. In other words: set the customer experience example.

9. Take a regular look in the mirror

Your role in customer signals management is often advisory. Impartial advice can only be given if you relinquish your own interests and perceptions. This keeps you from unnecessarily projecting ideas on other people and thus curbing their activeness. Be prepared to take a long hard look in the mirror, and regularly request honest feedback on your own performance.

All these preconditions are your framework for successful implementation of customer signals management. Last but not least, the final chapter provides inspiration in the form of lessons learned, which have proven to be successful interventions in practice.

10

LEARNING AND INSPIRING

He who seeks the error outside himself, will never be satisfied. He who seeks the error within himself and says: 'How stupid I have been', will be enriched by his experience.

— ALAIN

My eighteen years of practical experience with customer centricity and customer signals management have been very educational. Much of that material has already been discussed in this book. In order to inspire you and point you in the right direction, here are a number of examples which have worked well in practice to mobilize organizations and make a success of customer signals management.

1. Quality, old-style and new

An organization wanted to increase MT and board enthusiasm for customer signals management. It was to be introduced as a quality driver as it were. However, experience had shown the term 'quality' often elicits lukewarm reactions. This was solved by sketching a picture of 'old style quality' and 'new style quality' (see figure 10.1), followed by an indication of how customer signals management could put this new style quality into practice. And so a bridge was formed between the two parties and the MT became enthusiastic about implementing customer signals management.

2. Clear scope definition

An organization has many detailed customer processes and many channels, as well as being able to choose between customer contact, customer satisfaction, channels steering and continuous improve-

Image of old style quality at many companies	Image of new style quality at many companies
· quality drivers · PDCA · audits · rigid · long(er) processes · internal focus · supply steered	· focus on customer · learning from customers · continuous improvement · flexible · short-cyclic · external focus · demand steered

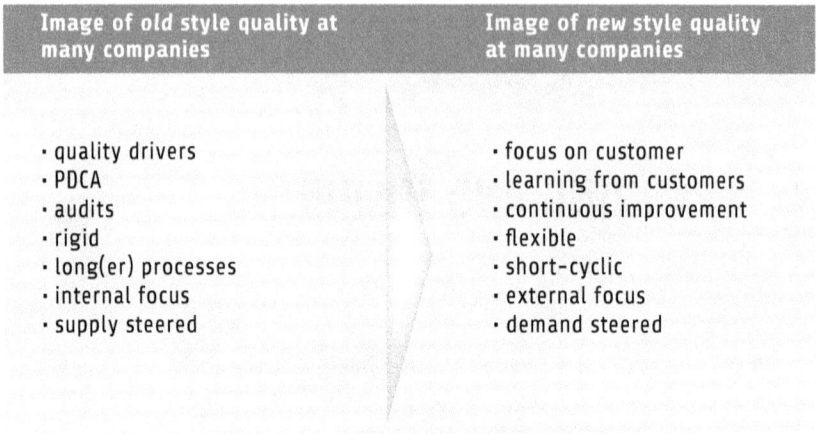

Figure 10.1 *Old style quality versus new style quality*

ment. You then run the risk of people losing their way in the maze of options and scope. Figure 10.2 clearly defines the total scope, where you now stand and how to move on.

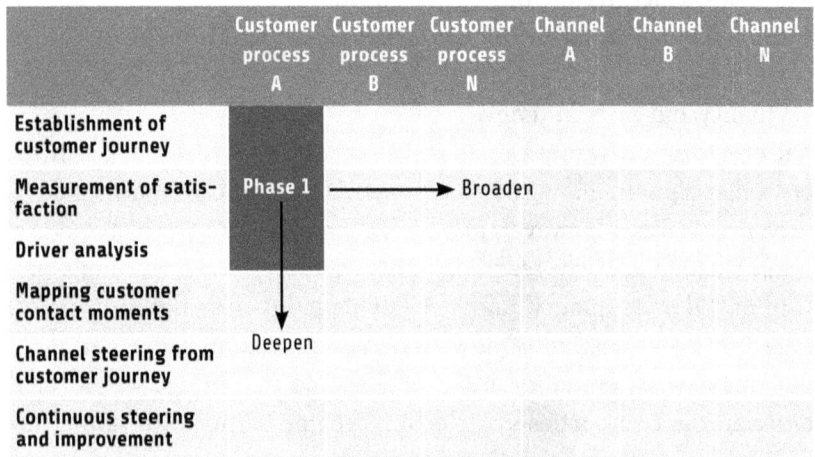

	Customer process A	Customer process B	Customer process N	Channel A	Channel B	Channel N
Establishment of customer journey						
Measurement of satisfaction	Phase 1	⟶ Broaden				
Driver analysis						
Mapping customer contact moments						
Channel steering from customer journey	Deepen					
Continuous steering and improvement						

Figure 10.2 *Scope of customer signals management*

In this example, phase 1 begins with a customer process for which you establish the detailed customer journey, measure the satisfaction and create the driver analysis. The organization then chooses how to continue. This can be horizontal broadening by designing the customer satisfaction surveys for the following customer processes and or/channels. Or vertical deepening by adding customer contact moments and channel steering as the basis for improvement of the satisfaction with the initial customer process. Or both of them parallel. There is no standard route in this sense: all three options can be effective, depending on the situation

3. Six weeks of ...
Employees often feel they have been thrown in at the deep end with all the new initiatives – especially those with customer contact. That is indeed often the case. In order to structure the process and thereby achieve better results, an organization applied a method of 'Six weeks of ...'. The target facing the organization was to reduce unnecessary customer contact. A central theme was introduced for the six weeks, focusing on a first-time fix for mutations, or steering customers towards online, for example. The employees received specific coaching on that theme during the six-week period, and the effect was measured at the end of that time. Six weeks of error-free mutations were shown to reduce repeat traffic by 4 percent. This approach is suitable for use in all kinds of departments in the organization.

4. No more than a one-pager
Every improvement to be made features a number of targets you wish to realize. It will hardly ever just be about customer satisfaction and customer contact moments. They must always be proportionate to other organization targets, such as costs, sales, et cetera. With these multiple sets of data to be monitored, you must take care not to drown in this ocean of figures. It is therefore useful to force yourself to gather all the relevant steering information per process or channel you wish to improve, on a one-pager. Simply thinking about this beforehand makes you more effective in deploying the correct points for improvement. As an example, figure 10.3 shows the 'becoming a customer' process of an insurance company, worked out on that single A4.

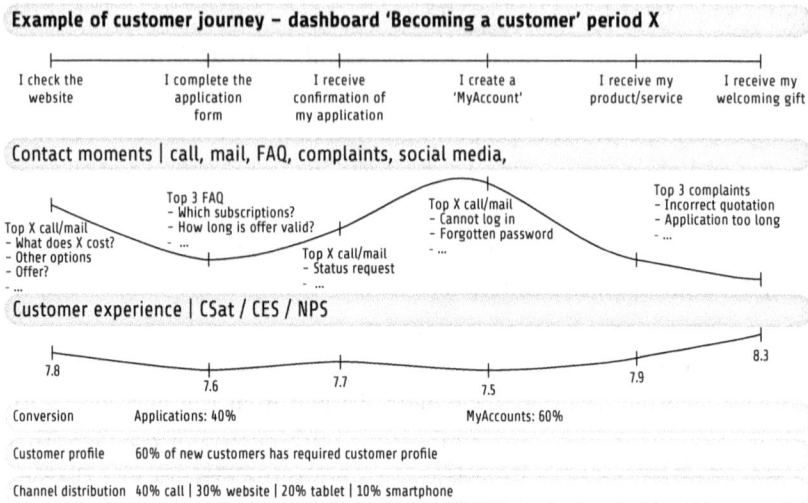

Figure 10.3 *Example of a single A4 with steering information for the 'Becoming a customer' process*

Customer journey and contact moments

As you know from the previous chapters, you can map out satisfaction and customer contact moments in this customer journey. It can be applied to all customer processes, though you also require specific process information.

Conversion

When becoming a customer, for example, this specific information concerns conversion. What percentage of customers starts to request product X and successfully buys the product (the so-called sales funnel)? And if they fail to do so, where do they drop out? And why? This is extremely relevant information in the purchasing process. Conversion can also be applied to service processes. What percentage of customers starts to change their data and successfully completes the process themselves? Where do they fail and why?

Customer profile

Also particularly important to commercial organizations, is the type of customer they attract. Are you aiming for the price-conscious customer and shoppers, or do you want to attract loyal customers with a higher customer value? Once again, you need to balance all the measuring information: if customers are extremely satisfied and you have a high conversion rate, but you are not attracting the customers you desire, then you need to adapt the process of becoming a customer. This will of course involve your total marketing mix (getting your campaigns right) and not simply the process. The total picture needs to add up. You therefore want to know what percentage of new customers has the desired profile.

Channel distribution
Most organizations want their customers to arrange services online where possible. That too must be monitored therefore, in this case by periodically comparing the percentage of applications made via telephone, e-mail and online, and determining whether this is moving in the right direction. If not, you need to take a closer look at why not. The insights gained from the other measuring indicators then help: customers are not satisfied, they make frequent calls, the conversion is not right. This can all contribute to the fact that customers prefer not to use the online channel.

5. Film clips of customers
What always works well and is not used nearly often enough, is to visualize what customers do and say. It is quite simple to generate photos and film clips of customer surveys nowadays. What a waste not to take advantage of getting more internal insight into images and sound relating to the organization's customers. A concrete example shows how this works well in practice, in the case of an organization whose website was under attack. The communication department had long since found that the current website was failing, but the MT did not recognize the urgency of having a new website developed. A usability study was then conducted among customers, and a film clip generated. The combination of customers stating that they could not find their way around it, and visualization of this in a twelve-minute clip, worked very well. The project to design a new website was commissioned shortly afterwards.

6. Brand, price and service perception

In an organization in which the board and management require a more strategic view of customer experience, the following approach is inspiring and stimulates the discussion of the necessary customer experience elements (see figure 10.4). In this view, customer experience is threefold: the service perception, price perception and brand perception. If you really want to take giant steps, make sure all three are mutually reinforcing, rather than them being individually steered, by various departments, as is now often the case. You need to interconnect the various departments responsible for these three elements.

Figure 10.4 *Three elements of customer experience*

Service perception
How can you get to grips with the perception of service? By using customer signals management to gain insight into the satisfaction drivers and by linking these to other signals received from customers. This element has already been discussed in detail in this book. However, there are two other elements which play a role: brand perception and price perception.

Brand perception
Almost all organizations have brand promises. How about Philips' 'Sense and Simplicity', Nokia's 'Connecting people' or AT&T's 'The world's networking company'? Much less common however is the translation of these brand promises into each step in the customer

journey, so that customers actually experience the promise in practice. 'The world's networking company' says something about the communication on the website, about the channels offered by the organization and about the way in which the organization conducts dialogs. First and foremost as a customer, I expect innovation from such a brand promise, therefore also in the service I receive. In that sense, the brand perception should actually be translated into design principles to be applied in each step of the customer journey. Per step, you decide how to fulfill the brand promise. This is often not the case at all, and even if it is done, it is too superficial and not translated into the detailed customer journey. There is much to gain, if you can connect your service and brand perceptions.

Price perception
The price I pay as a customer is also a driver of my experience. At Walmart, I know I can expect the lowest price, and a certain experience in the store. When buying an Apple laptop, I know that I'm paying substantially more than I would for another brand, even though there are very few differences, technically speaking. This clearly shows how brand perception can dictate the asking price. The crux here is that the price is linked to those elements which customers believe to be important. If a customer has no idea what he is paying for (as in car insurance, for example), he will quite simply search for the lowest price. The product is too complex to compare other elements.

However, you can also think in terms of developing relevant services which customers consider valuable. Once again, you can make a study of this: which services do you believe relevant and what is their value? Like the other two, the gain is once again found in the connection. As we often see: ticking the individual 'boxes' (service perception, brand perception and price perception) is much less effective than when you can always tick all the boxes (the customer experience).

Here are five tips to get you started:
1. Measure which service elements customers really believe to be important.
2. Translate the brand values into the service and price offered.

3. Apply the relevant service perception scores in your brand perception manifestations.
4. Link your pricing to those elements which customers believe important.
5. Translate a product feature into a customer-relevant feature (one which the customer understands).

7. Create internships

When applying customer signals management, you want people to become aware of the customer journey. Employees and managers in the various departments do not have enough insight into the actions of other departments in the journey, from the customer's perspective. The HR policy should therefore include one 'fieldwork' day per month, in which each employee, team leader, manager and director spends a day with a colleague from one of the other departments in the journey. These people can subsequently be connected, so that they can always have contact after their training day if there are issues to be solved in the customer journey. And so you link crucial people in the end-to-end journey, and avoid them being able to hide behind 'us and them' behavior.

And finally: stay creative and experiment!

The best way of mobilizing an organization once you have drawn people's attention to customer centricity, is to keep the process fun and inspiring. So challenge yourself, keep looking for new creative methods and techniques and don't be afraid to step out of your comfort zone. After all you've read so far, you will be able to implement customer signals management in any organization. I hope you will enjoy the challenges; let's make this a more customer-centric world!

ACKNOWLEDGEMENTS

This book is the precious result of many years of pioneering. I have been fascinated to work with organizations in their day-to-day practice, while also undertaking scientific research and a healthy portion of soul-searching on a personal level. It is thanks to the interaction and connection with others that I have arrived here today, and I consider myself blessed. All the people I have encountered over the past 38 years have played their own role, knowingly or unknowingly. I would like to mention a number of them individually.

To begin with, my employers and clients over the years. My employers PinkRoccade e-Finance, Capgemini and the Delta Lloyd Group for allowing me more than my fair share of freedom to continually develop myself and my vision of this field. My clients for their trust in embarking on this adventure with me and the openness they have shown in our ongoing peer reflection.

In the scientific world, I cannot of course help but mention Professor Dr. José Bloemer. We shared 6.5 years of doctoral research ups and downs – one of the results of which was an extremely poignant laudation during my Ph.D. ceremony, which I still occasionally re-read if I feel the need for goose bumps.

Specifically for the production of the book, I would like to thank my co-readers: Merième, Miranda, Niels, Ljiljana, Paul and Dave. Thanks to your feedback, the book has become not 100% but 200% of all I had hoped for.

Besides thanking a number of special friends and my sister, I must conclude by expressing my everlasting gratitude to my husband. Words can never be enough to express how important you are to me. I look forward to many more years of traveling together!

ABOUT THE AUTHOR

Zanna van der Aa (1978) has more than fifteen years of experience in the field of customer and employee experience. She has an internationally proven track record in helping organizations to be measurably successful in the field of experience. She graduated in Business Computer Science and subsequently also in Marketing, allowing her to effectively link two increasingly cohesive professional fields. The 2005 to 2012 period was spent on doctoral research at Radboud University in Nijmegen, next to her job as a consultant in customer experience at Capgemini. At work, she regularly spreads "the word" in lectures, magazines and blogs.

"Bringing the customer inside, to create excellent services outside." That is her day-to-day business. Call it customer experience, customer engagement, omni channel, change management... or simply call it common sense. It's actually very simple: imagine how you would treat a good friend, and you're well on your way. Practical realization of the method is extremely complex however, which is why she loves the challenge of this field.

Questions put to her by organizations include:
* if I've got a hundred grand to spend, what's my best investment to improve customer experience?

- how can I gear my KPIs to what customers really believe important?
- how can I continuously steer customer satisfaction and/or employee satisfaction?
- how do I reduce unnecessary customer contact?
- how can I get my entire organization working from the customer's perspective?
- how can I continuously improve services from the customer's point of view, with measurable success?
- how can I steer effectively towards online?
- how do I get the entire organization on board the required change without it turning into a lengthy and laborious uphill struggle?

For more information, check out her LinkedIn profile (linkedin.com/in/zannavdun) or her website zannavanderaa.com.

BIBLIOGRAPHY

Aa, van der, Z. (2011). *The Role of the Customer Contact Center in Relationship Marketing*. Nijmegen: PhD thesis Radboud University.

Barlow, J. and Moller, C., (1996). *Een klacht... een geschenk uit de hemel én een effectief strategisch middel*. Amsterdam: Uitgeverij Contact.

Dixon, M. and Toman, N., (2013). *The Effortless Experience*. Amsterdam: Penguin Books Ltd.

Fornell, C. (2008). *The Satisfied Customer*. New York: Palgrave USA.

Gilmore, J.H. and Pine, J. (1999). *The Experience Economy*. Brighton: Harvard Business Review Press.

Heskett, J.L. and Sasser, W.E. (1997). *The Service Profit Chain*. New York: Simon & Schuster.

Herzberg, F. (1966). *Work and the Nature of Man*. New York: Staples Press.

Kano, N. (1984). Attractive quality and must be quality. *Hinshitsu {Quality}*, 14(2), pp. 147-156.

Matzler, K., Fuchs, M., and Schubert, A.K. (2004). Employee Satisfaction: Does KANO's model apply? *Total Quality Management,* 15(9-10), pp. 1179-1198.

Reichheld, F. F. (1996). *The Loyalty Effect.* New York: Harvard Business School Publishing.

Reichheld, F.F. (2006). *The Ultimate Question.* New York: Harvard Business School Publishing.